· GARDENING · BY · DES[IGN]

WINDOW
BOXES

· MARTIN · BAXENDALE ·

Ward Lock Limited · London

©Ward Lock Limited 1986

First published in Great Britain in 1986
by Ward Lock Limited, 8 Clifford Street
London W1X 1RB An Egmont Company

House editor Denis Ingram
Designed by Niki fforde

Text set in Bembo Roman
by HBM Typesetting Limited, Chorley, Lancashire

Printed and bound in Spain by Graficas Reunidas

British Library Cataloguing in Publication Data

Baxendale, Martin
Window boxes
1. Window-gardening
I. Title
635.9'65   SB419

ISBN 0-7063-6451-1

CONTENTS

PREFACE

Nothing brings a building to life quite like a cheerful display of window boxes and hanging baskets frothing over with bright summer colour and fresh greenery, be it a house, apartment block, store-front or city office; and it really is so easy to brighten up your home or workplace in this delightful way.

Window boxes and hanging baskets are of course particularly appealing to gardenless apartment-dwellers, but they'll enhance any home, softening the hard lines of stone, brick or concrete with cascades of foliage and flower, lighting up dull corners and generally helping to 'clothe' the house. As for those offices and store-fronts, flowers and refreshing greenery are as welcome at work and on the dusty main streets of towns and cities as in the garden or outside the apartment window.

Creating truly stunning displays, however, isn't just a matter of haphazardly throwing a few plants together and hoping for the best. As in any form of gardening, the more care you take over planning and design, the better the effect will be.

Nor are window-box gardens just for summer flowers, of course. With carefully thought-out seasonal planting schemes, your windows and walls can be colourful and interesting right through spring, summer, autumn and winter; or evergreen plants can be chosen to create permanent effects that look good all year round yet require a minimum of maintenance. Window boxes can be useful too, growing herbs, fresh fruits and vegetables for the apartment kitchen. So take another look at the house frontage, lean out of the apartment or office window, walk around the front of the store—and start planning.

M.B.

ACKNOWLEDGEMENTS

All the colour photographs were taken by Bob Challinor.

The publishers are grateful to the following persons for
kindly granting permission for photographs of their window boxes to be taken:
Miss J. Egerton-Warburton (p54) and Mrs S. Gosselin (pp59, 62 & 63).

All the line drawings were drawn by Nils Solberg.

1

PLANNING AND DESIGN

THE CONTAINERS

The first step towards creating handsome window garden displays is, naturally, to choose your containers; and there is a vast range available, from highly ornate troughs to the simplest of wooden boxes.

Like many gardeners, I prefer my plants to be the main attraction, rather than their containers; so for preference I would usually go for something fairly simple and plain which won't fight with the flowers for attention. It's all a matter of personal taste, but do remember that a highly decorated or brightly coloured box may appeal when seen in the store but look very unnatural and clash with the flowers when planted up.

It's also best if the window boxes don't clash too much with the style of the building, either. The one situation where you could perhaps get away with having very intricately designed and ornamented containers would be where the architecture is equally ornate; for example, in a Spanish style, against which more intricate boxes wouldn't seem so out of place.

However, something plain and more utilitarian, with clean lines and a neutral colour, would better suit the vast majority of buildings (particularly modern ones) as well as setting the plants off to better effect.

Colour

Speaking of colour, you can of course select or paint containers to match the paintwork of your windows, and this can look very effective, but bear in mind that white boxes will need annual repainting and regular cleaning (particularly in urban areas), otherwise they'll quickly become dirty and unsightly.

Boxes may also be chosen or painted in a colour to blend with the walls (e.g. brick-red, stone hues, or to match coloured rendering or painted walls) and this is especially effective where the containers are to be fixed on brackets just below the windows, rather than actually on the sills.

If in doubt, play safe and opt for subdued tints like dark green, beige, brown or plain varnished timber, all of which will offset plants and flowers well. Bear in mind also, if you're hand-painting, that a matt finish generally looks more subdued and blends in better than a high-gloss paint (unless you're matching it to existing glossy paintwork.)

Material

Plastic troughs are light to handle and should have a long life provided they're made from good heavy-duty material; very thin and flimsy poor quality plastics may quickly become brittle in sunlight, making them prone to cracking and breakage.

Be wary when buying decorative metal containers as well. Wrought iron and steel may be robust but can quickly start to rust unless well coated with paint or plastic against the elements, and no-one wants unsightly rain-washed rust stains disfiguring the house; particularly where the walls are white or of a very pale colouring.

Glass fibre is a good choice, tough and very long-lasting, and unglazed eathenware pottery troughs look very classy.

I really don't think you can beat good old-fashioned

timber; it's comparatively inexpensive (especially if you build your own boxes); it lasts well if treated inside with preservative; it's easily painted to suit your requirements and looks particularly good when clear varnished to make a handsome feature of the wood grain. If you can obtain rough-cut planks complete with bark edgings, or a bark-covered facing timber, these will give your window gardens a particularly attractive rustic look: lovely on an older house, and an interesting natural contrast to an ultra-modern frontage or a large picture window.

Size

The box should be as large as the window ledge will allow. The more planting compost it holds, the longer it'll take to dry out between waterings, which means less work and worry; and of course you'll be able to squeeze in more plants in greater variety for a really marvellous display.

Shallow containers should be avoided wherever possible, as these dry out fastest of all and therefore demand very frequent watering. Anything shallower than 15 cm (6 in) is likely to cause trouble, and 20 cm (8 in) or more is better.

You needn't settle for a very narrow box even if the window sill is shallow; your container can project out a little way from the sill without looking odd, and on an extremely narrow ledge a wide box can be supported at the front with wall brackets (see 'Positioning and fixing' below).

POTS AND REMOVABLE LINERS

There are two basic ways to use window boxes; simply filled with growing compost and planted up, or as containers to hold removable liners or pot-grown plants (Fig. 1). The first option is the most straightforward, but the second does allow for quicker and simpler seasonal changes and alterations to the display.

Boxes with removable liners certainly make life easy for the window-gardener. When the spring display starts to fade, for example, the inner liner containing the spring flowers is easily removed, speedily making way for a fresh liner full of plants for summer, and so on through the seasons. Even permanent displays of perennial plants may, in this way, be moved around from one window box to another for variety and a change of scene; or permanent plantings may be removed for ease of weeding, replanting and other maintenance tasks.

Having said that, window boxes with removable liners are probably most useful to someone with a garden, yard or glasshouse space where liners full of seasonal plants may be continually grown on in readiness for a quick change-over. In an apartment, with no facilities for this kind of conveyor-belt planning and preparation, removable liners aren't as much of an asset.

Growing pot plants free-standing on window ledges is always hazardous, with every strong gust of wind (or careless movement when watering) likely to send them crashing to the ground–a very real danger in the case of high windows, when the risk of broken heads below must be taken into consideration. They'll be perfectly safe, however, in a securely fixed window box and will offer the same quick-change benefits as removable liners; in fact, even more so.

Plunge material

Pot plants may be simply placed in the window box, but they're better plunged in a water-retentive material like peat or one of the newer lightweight man-made plunging materials. This will help to keep the individual pots cool and moist, reducing the need for hand-watering.

Note that the plunge material should be watered at the same time as the pots, so that it acts as a reservoir of moisture which can be taken up through the bases of the pots; dry plunge material may actually draw water out of the pots, having the opposite effect to the one desired.

Fig. 1b. Using a box to hold pot-grown plants is a versatile method of window gardening. Swopping plants around for seasonal interest is quick and easy.

Fig. 1a. With removable liners to fit your window boxes, changing the plants for colour in different seasons becomes a simple matter. Buy two liners per box, and you can always have the next season's flowers growing on in advance, ready for a quick change-over.

If the plunge material is deep enough to just cover and hide the rims of the pots, so that the plants appear to be growing in the box, the effect will be that much more attractive.

Making your own

Home-made timber boxes couldn't be simpler, demanding little in the way of carpentry skills, and they can of course be tailored to fit your individual windows.

Inexpensive softwood (e.g. pine) is quite acceptable and long-lasting if treated with preservative and given

a fresh coat of paint or varnish annually. Varnished hardwood boxes look very classy and have a long life but are naturally far more costly.

A very simple straight-sided 'ammunition box' shape is perfectly good and easy to construct, but sloping the front out a little towards the top by cutting the end-pieces at an angle (Fig. 2) produces a slightly more pleasing effect. An angled front piece allows for a larger planting area of compost at the top of the box, and a larger surface area for catching valuable rain-water. It also permits trailing plants and flowers to cascade over the front in a freer and more attractive way.

Don't forget to drill drainage holes in the base, preferably about 2 cm (¾ in) in diameter so that they won't become blocked up with compost; and nail or screw a small strip of timber to each end of the base to act as feet and raise the box off the ledge, again to ensure free drainage of excess water.

Text continues on p. 12

An oasis of colour and greenery on a city street: note the window boxes and baskets arranged so that they drape the frontage with a cascading ribbon of flowers and foliage, crossing and breaking up the hard architectural lines.

Even the most handsome of doorways looks more attractive framed with colourful hanging baskets; here planted with bright red and pink pelargoniums.

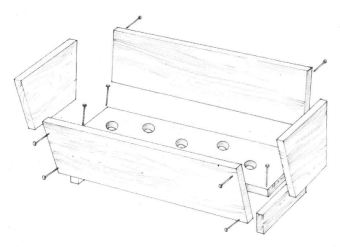

Fig. 2. Constructing a home-made window box: use timber 1.9–2.5 cm (¾–1 in) thick. Be sure to drill large drainage holes in the base, and tack strips of timber under the base to raise it off the window ledge.

Fig. 3. Make sure that window boxes are safely secured, particularly on high ledges. The easiest way is to screw eye-hooks into each end of the box, attaching these with wire to eye-hooks screwed into the window frame.

Treat the inside of the box with a couple of coats of preservative, using one that's recommended by the manufacturer as not harmful to plants (e.g. those containing copper napthenate; your local garden or hardware store should be able to advise on available brands.) Store-bought wooden window boxes should have been pretreated in this way, but it's worthwhile checking; and, in any case, only one coat may have been given, so an extra treatment won't do any harm. Emptying, cleaning and reapplying preservative once a year when replanting will help to ensure many years of useful life from your boxes.

Protect the outside of home-made containers with a couple of coats of exterior quality varnish or paint, taking care to work this thoroughly into the joints. Sand down any rough surfaces before painting. Repaint or varnish annually for long life.

POSITIONING AND FIXING

Where the box can be placed on the window ledge, this obviously makes thing very easy, but even here, it's best to secure the container to ensure that it can't be accidentally knocked to the ground; and this is particularly important, as a safety factor, with high windows. Eye-and-hook catches may be fitted to the ends of the box and the sides of the window, or simple eye-hooks screwed into the window frame and box may be connected by strong wire (Fig. 3).

Should the window ledge be rather narrow, an overhanging box may be secured by attaching metal brackets to the base at the front, bending these around the sill and fixing them to the wall below (Fig. 4).

Where the ledge is virtually non-existent, the box will have to be attached with brackets to the wall just below the window. This is also where the box will have to be located if the window opens outwards, making it impossible to place anything on the ledge outside. Alternatively, under ground-floor windows, boxes may be supported on wooden legs (Fig. 5).

Don't be put off the idea of window gardens if this is the situation that you face. It's not at all difficult, using an ordinary power drill with a masonry bit, screws and wall plugs, to fit suitable brackets; and if you can't tackle it yourself, any handyman should be able to do the job for you quickly and inexpensively.

Using wall brackets, it's equally easy to fit hanging baskets above and alongside windows, to add yet another interesting dimension to your window gardens; but more on that later.

As to aspect, sunny windows are the ideal sites for box gardens, since the majority of plants do best with

Fig. 4. On a narrow ledge, the box may be allowed to overhang provided it is secured with brackets and timber blocks to the wall beneath.

Fig. 5a. Where the ledge is extremely narrow, or where there is no ledge at all, a box may be fixed with brackets to the wall just below the window.

Fig. 5b. Alternatively, boxes may be raised up on supports to the level of a ground-floor window, where the ledge is very narrow.

Text continues on p. 16

All the ingredients of a classical arrangement: a tall plant hugging close to one side of the window, lower-growing pelargoniums in the centre, all balanced by the trailing lobelias below.

Simple timber boxes are an excellent choice; a natural setting for the flowers, neutral in colour and perfect for buildings with a period character that might be spoiled by the intrusion of modern plastic containers.

15

plenty of sunlight. If you're planning just one or two window boxes, choose your sunniest windows. However, even the gloomiest sunless situations can be brightened up, using a selection of shade-loving and shade-tolerant plants (see 'Plants for Shade' at the end of this chapter).

PLANTING SCHEMES

The first thing to decide, after buying or constructing the containers, is the type of planting schemes that you want: whether seasonal 'bedding' with spring flowers followed by a fresh set of plants for summer colour, and so on through the year; or fairly permanent planting schemes, comprising evergreen perennials for year-round interest; or herbs, fruits and vegetables.

Naturally, if you're planning more than one window garden then you can go for a variety, some with seasonal plants and some for permanent effects. It's quite possible to mix temporary seasonal flowers for summer with such things as herbs, small fruit plants and vegetables all in the same box.

What you decide will depend on various factors—how much work you're prepared to put in on emptying and refilling the boxes for different seasons; whether you'd prefer to just plant up the once, with things for a long-lasting effect; whether you want to grow fresh produce for the kitchen, and so on. Frequent replanting with temporary plants does involve more work, but means lots of bright colour. Permanent plantings tend to be rather less colourful, with a show of flowers one month, a gap, some more colour later, and with handsome evergreen foliage playing a major role.

The one strong recommendation that I'd make is to be adventurous and try as many different types of planting schemes and as many different types of plants as possible—variety being the spice of life, after all.

Whatever you're going to grow, the most important thing is to spend plenty of time on planning and design before you pick up a trowel, and before you buy a single plant; just as you would before setting out to create a full-size garden. The points to bear in mind are indeed virtually the same as those that apply to larger-scale gardening.

The first point, and probably the most important, is to plan for a constant succession of colour and interest, ideally right around the year. With seasonal replantings—a fresh set of temporary annuals, bulbs and suchlike for spring, summer, autumn and winter—this is easily achieved, but it does involve planning ahead; making out lists well in advance, of plants and bulbs to be bought, and seeds to be sown, in readiness for a quick change-over at the end of each season's display.

The best way is to work out, on paper, a series of planting schemes for the whole year. This will then, at least, act as a basic planting timetable on which you can elaborate or improvise if you wish, as each season comes around and replanting time approaches.

With permanent displays of perennial plants, it means choosing attractive evergreens for constant foliage interest, preferably with contrasting leaf shapes and tints. It also means trying to select your plants so that you'll have at least some flowers in each season.

There's a limit to what can be done in a small container, but even in a tiny window box it should be possible to include at least one plant for spring flowers, another for summer, one for autumn and yet another for winter. It also helps to select plants which bloom over a long period within their appointed season. We'll be looking at plant selection for different times of year and for long-flowering later. For now, some more basic guidelines on good design.

Height

As in any garden, variations in height, scale and form are essential for an interesting and eye-catching effect. The last thing you want to end up with is a box boringly filled with plants all of the same height and habit of growth. Think of the window box as a garden bed or border, and plan for as much variety as possible.

One or two tall 'spot' plants are essential, as focal points for the whole arrangement. In a garden border, these would be towards the back, with smaller plants grading down towards the front. But in a window box the approach has to be rather different. You don't want to block the view and the daylight from the window too much, so the best place for the tallest things is at the sides, with the rest of the plants getting gradually smaller towards the centre. You could place two tall plants of the same type and height, one at each side of the window, but even here it's that bit more interesting

if you can get a little extra variation into the design.

A classic arrangement would be to place a very tall plant on one side as the main focal point, grading down to smaller plants and then up again a little to a medium-tall specimen on the other side. In this arrangement, as in a well structured painting, the eye is caught by the tallest plant to one side, and then drawn in towards the centre of the feature by the curving downward line; an effect that's natural and pleasing to the eye.

Much depends on the shape and size of the window, of course. A very wide window, for example, could accommodate tall plants (and possibly a number of them in a group) on both sides, without blocking out the view and daylight excessively.

Naturally, a very long window box could accommodate additional slight 'ups-and-downs' of height variation between these two extremities. However, plants towards the centre should still not be too tall, and certainly not taller than those to the sides—the aim should always be to enhance and 'frame' the window with flowers and foliage, not to obscure it with a tall mass in the middle.

A very narrow window, on the other hand, might only be wide enough to take a single tall plant to one side, with the other plants grading down in height towards the opposite corner.

Climbing plants are also useful for adding height towards the sides of the box, supported on canes or perhaps on a narrow wooden or plastic trellis attached to the inside of the window. Very tall, narrow windows in particular cry out for perennial or annual climbers to scramble up them (Fig. 6); and in such a situation, you'll often find that climbers make better 'height' plants, clinging close to the side of the window and cutting out less light than a tall, bushy plant.

Large windows which are both tall and wide offer the greatest possibilities for exciting displays using all of these elements; climbers scrambling all the way up the sides, tall bushy plants inside these, curving down to ever smaller things, and possibly a few more medium-height plants for added variety (see Fig. 7 for the effect of height variations).

Fig. 6. A climbing plant trained on canes or a trellis to one side of the window will add greatly to the character and appeal of your window box garden. It will add extra height to the display without blocking the window excessively.

Text continues on p. 20

The exotic, large-flowered petunias are ideal for window gardens, particularly the pink, violet-blue and red 'Cascade' strains.

Tubs are also useful when it comes to decking the house with summer colour; especially where paving or concrete makes it impossible to plant at the base of a wall.

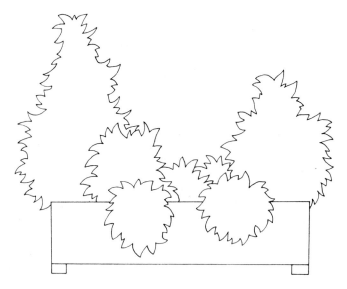

Fig. 7. A classic window box planting design; using a tall focal plant to one side, grading down to smaller plants in the centre (to avoid blocking the light and view through the window) and finally rising up again at the other end to a medium-height plant; the whole arrangement forming a pleasing curve.

Trailing plants

Trailers are just as vital, spilling out of the box and cascading downwards; and without at least one trailing plant, no window garden could be complete. They add an exotic 'jungly' touch and (equally important) they help to balance the feature, offsetting the height of the taller plants and climbers above; a window garden without trailers tends to look top-heavy, and (vice versa) one with trailers and no tall plants can appear bottom-heavy.

Speaking of climbers and trailers, it's interesting to experiment with mixed plantings for unusual effects. For example, two different types of climbing plants may be placed close together to scramble up through one another. Perhaps an ivy with handsome glossy foliage, and a sweet pea to twine up through this, the flowers peeping out from amongst the ivy leaves. Or, in a permanent planting of evergreens, you could use two different types of ivy, one with dark green leaves and the other a golden or silver variegated variety; or one large-leaved and the other with small leaves. Remember that ivies can be used both as climbers and as trailers.

With trailers, the same sort of mix-and-match principle may be tried. Put one trailing plant at the front of the window box and a second (different) one just behind it, to grow through the first plant so that their trailing leaves or flowers cascade out of the box intertwined.

Colour

With flowering plants, try to match the flower colour so that they go well together, otherwise the whole effect will be spoiled.

Don't forget that foliage plants can also play an important role, not just in permanent evergreen plantings but also in seasonal arrangements where variegated leaves, silver foliage and other colourful leaf tints may greatly add to the overall effect. More on these later.

On a more general point, in larger-scale gardening, groups of plants of the same type massed together often look better than a patchwork mixture made up of single plants of different kinds. This principle, too, can sometimes be applied to window boxes, bearing in mind the limitations of space. The smallest window gardens may only offer space for one tall focal plant or climber, one or two smaller bushy things and a single trailer, but where space permits, in large boxes, arranging the plants in groups of two or three of the same kind and colour together does produce a very bold and pleasing effect.

You'll have noted from some of the above design suggestions that much depends on the size and shape of the window, and on the size of the box, much the same as in a garden, where layout and planting are often greatly influenced by the shape, size and situation of the plot.

So let's now take a look at other ways in which window garden displays can be designed to suit, and to enhance, different types of situation.

Site of container

For a start, what difference does it make to the planting scheme whether the window box sits on the ledge or is fixed to the wall beneath? I've already mentioned placing low-growing plants towards the centre of the display, to avoid blocking the window too much. Bearing this in mind, it's obvious that these central flowers can be taller in a box fitted below the window than in one sitting on the ledge; and all the plants could be that little bit taller if you so wished.

Indeed, a 'low-slung' box just below the ledge will allow a wider range of plants to be grown, bringing in the possibility of taller things that might not suit a window-ledge box. Should you have a hankering for certain types of taller flowers, say tall growing bulbs like lilies for summer, then it might well be a good idea to purposely site the container under the ledge (Fig. 8).

There is, however, an important point that affects this question of plant height greatly, and which hasn't yet been mentioned: whether the window is exposed and windy or well sheltered. Naturally, a window garden in a particularly windy situation is best planted mostly with very short, sturdy things that will stand up to constant buffeting without flopping over or snapping off at the stem. This applies particularly to windows above the ground floor, and especially to high windows facing the wind funnels of canyon-like city streets.

Ground-floor windows tend to be less windy, since wind speeds are always slower at lower levels and there's usually more wind shelter around. Here taller plants and bulbs should be safer, except in a very exposed position.

Plants for air pollution

In city areas subject to heavy and frequent air pollution, it pays to include at least some really tough, pollution-tolerant plants in the window display.

Fig. 8. Fixing a box with brackets below a window will often allow quite tall plants to be used; these sturdy 'Mid-Century' hybrid lilies, for example. If you wish to grow taller plants, you might like to deliberately site your box in this position, whether you have a window ledge or not.

Plants which will stand heavy air pollution include: *Iberis* (candytuft), both the annual *I. umbellata* varieties, and the perennial rock garden species and varieties like *I. sempervirens*; ivies for foliage interest, as climbers and trailing plants; *Dianthus* (pinks); primroses and polyanthus primroses; dwarf *Euonymus fortunei* varieties, like 'Silver Queen' for colourful foliage; dwarf rhododendrons or evergreen azaleas; and virtually all bulbs (spring, summer, autumn and winter flowering).

Colour effects

Flower and foliage colours should also, to some extent at least, be selected with the situation and surroundings

Text continues on p. 24

Fuchsias, petunias, pelargoniums and lobelias mingle in a froth of summer colour.

No ledge to this bay window, so the owner makes sensible use of the level window-roof instead.

in mind. Most importantly, the colours shouldn't blend in with the background too much. To take an extreme example, white flowers are unlikely to stand out and show up to best effect if they trail over the edge of the window box with a brilliant white painted wall as a background.

In general, pale flowers and light foliage tints look best contrasted against a darker background; yellows, pinks and whites against dark brick or stone, for example. And vice versa: deeper colours like hot reds, blues, purples and violets stand out better against a light background, like a white or pastel colour-washed wall. This is worth bearing in mind particularly when choosing plants to trail over the edges or front of a box, and with plants to grow up the sides of the window.

Darker coloured flowers also tend to show up best in sunny situations, where sunlight streaming through their petals will light them up and really bring them to life; in shade, they may look duller and less lively. The best flower colours for brightening up gloomy shady windows are the gleaming paler ones.

Plants for shade

Speaking of shade, sunless window gardens do require more thought than sunny ones, since so many plants grow too weakly and spindly or refuse to flower properly in shade. As a general guide, the following is a selection of plants which will tolerate or do well in this kind of situation. For further information, see the plant lists.

Bulbs, corms and tubers: tuberous anemones, tuberous begonias, *Chionodoxa, Colchicum,* crocus, hardy cyclamen, *Eranthis, Galanthus, Hyacinthus, Ipheion, Narcissus, Scilla.*

Annuals: *Begonia semperflorens, Calceolaria* (slipper flower), *Impatiens* (busy Lizzie), *Lobelia, Malcolmia* (Virginia stock), *Mimulus* (monkey flower), *Nemophila* (baby blue eyes), *Viola* (pansy).

Perennials and dwarf shrubby plants: *Hedera* (ivies), *Primula* (primroses and polyanthus), fuchsias, ferns, dwarf rhododendrons, dwarf evergreen azaleas, *Lysimachia nummularia* (creeping Jenny).

2

USING TEMPORARY SEASONAL PLANTS

Summer is the season that most people associate with window box displays more than any other time of year; and this is indeed when they're at their best, brimming over with the brilliant, long-lasting colour of exotic-flowered annuals and tender bedding plants like fuchsias and pelargoniums, but it would be a shame to leave the boxes bare and empty for the rest of the year.

Exactly how the planting timetable for the year is worked out depends to some extent on whether plants and bulbs are being grown direct in the boxes, or in removable liners and pots. Using liners and pots inside the boxes does allow more flexibility, as I've already mentioned. Let's go through the seasons and see what we can use to brighten up our windows, and when.

SUMMER

Annuals are the mainstay of the summer display (Fig. 9), backed up by one or two frost-tender perennials and perhaps some of the neater summer bulbs.

Sowing time for annuals to flower in summer is from late winter to early spring. Hardy annuals may be sown direct into the box; but they get off to a faster start, make larger plants and flower earlier if sown in pots or trays under·cover, to be planted out once growing strongly. Half-hardy annuals must be sown in warmth and planted out after the spring frosts are over (except in areas with a very mild, frost-free climate). A glasshouse is invaluable for seed-sowing and growing-on, but it's quite possible to raise seedlings indoors on a windowsill.

Fig. 9. An example of a well-planted seasonal display for summer, with a balanced mix of tall plants (fuchsia, *left,* calceolaria, *centre* and pelargonium, *right*) lower, bushy plants (sweet alyssum and impatiens, *right centre*) and trailers (lobelia, *left* and nasturtium, *right*).

Alternatively, young annual plants may be bought from market stalls, gardening stores and nurseries in late spring or early summer, ready for immediate planting. However, the range available is usually limited, and you can choose from a wider and more exciting selection if you raise your own from seed.

Annuals

Many annual plants are too large for window boxes, but the following is a selection of suitable types:

TRAILING PLANTS

Alyssum maritimum, *Lobelia*, *Impatiens* (pendulous varieties), *Lathyrus* (sweat pea), *Petunia*, *Thunbergia* (black-eyed Susan), *Tropaeolum* (nasturtium).

NEAT, BUSHY PLANTS

Ageratum, *Anchusa capensis* 'Blue Angel', dwarf *Antirrhinum* (snapdragon), *Begonia semperflorens*, *Lobelia*, *Calceolaria* (slipper flower), dwarf bedding dahlias, *Alyssum*, *Dimorphotheca* (star of the veldt), *Eschscholzia* (Californian poppy), *Gazania*, dwarf *Godetia*, *Iberis* (candytuft), dwarf bushy *Impatiens*, *Limnanthes* (poached egg plant), *Malcolmia* (Virginia stock), *Mesembryanthemum* (Livingstone daisy), *Mimulus*, *Petunia*, *Nemophila* (baby blue eyes), *Nemesia*, dwarf *Nicotiana* (tobacco plant), dwarf annual phlox, *Salvia*, dwarf *Tagetes* (African and French marigolds), dwarf *Zinnia*.

Some of the above are available in taller varieties or strains suitable for adding height to the display, notably the salvias, *Antirrhinum*, bedding dahlia, *Godetia*, *Nicotiana*, *Tagetes* and *Zinnia*. But many of the taller annuals may be tried as feature plants.

CLIMBERS

Lathyrus (sweat pea), *Ipomoea* (morning glory), *Cobaea* (cathedral bells), *Eccremocarpus scaber* (Chilean glory flower), *Thunbergia*, *Nasturtium* (climbing varieties).

Perennials

Tender glasshouse-type perennials, like the fuchsias and pelargoniums, may be planted direct into boxes, or they may be grown in pots, to be plunged or placed in the box for the summer. In all but the warmest frost-free areas, these plants must be kept on an indoor windowsill or in a heated glasshouse during winter. Growing them in pots as mentioned above makes this seasonal move easier; but even when they're planted direct into the boxes, it doesn't take long to simply knock some of the growing compost off their roots in late autumn and pot them up for the winter.

Young, bushy plants may be bought, along with annual seedlings, from market stalls, gardening stores and nurseries in late spring and early summer. They shouldn't be planted out in the window gardens until all danger of late spring frost is over.

Most may be propagated from cuttings of non-flowering shoots in spring or early summer. Pelargoniums and dwarf dahlias may also be raised from seed sown in heat during late winter, to flower the same year.

Speaking of raising tender bedding perennials from seed, dwarf dahlia seed is often sold as a half-hardy annual; but the tuberous roots are perennial and can be lifted and stored frost-free in pots of compost during winter, to flower again in future years.

Long-flowering dwarf dahlias suitable for window boxes are available in double and single flowered strains; go for the neatest types that don't grow above 30 cm (12 in).

Begonia semperflorens, usually sold as an annual, can also be potted up and kept indoors or in a frost-free glasshouse during winter.

Pelargoniums

Pelargoniums are probably the all-time favourites for summer colour in window boxes, and their hot reds and bright candy pinks are unbeatable for a truly eye-catching show. All have handsome foliage, often attractively marked with red-purple or other tints. Tall varieties are stunning 'height' plants, and the newer miniature strains of pelargonium are particularly suitable for even the smallest window box; some produce dainty small flowers, others are as large in bloom as the tallest strains and varieties.

The ordinary bedding pelargoniums are easy and flower freely over a long period. The rather fancier regal or show varieties with their jagged-edged leaves and ruffled flowers are better as indoor or greenhouse plants except in the warmest areas.

Luckily the ivy-leaved *Pelargonium peltatum* is as easy

Pot holders are an excellent alternative to hanging baskets, and these black-painted iron fixtures are perfectly in keeping with the period character of the cottage.

to grow and as free-flowering as the bedding varieties. This is a superb trailing plant with lovely ivy-like foliage and flowers of red, pink, white or mauve. The variety 'L'Elegante' is particularly attractive, with its small white flowers and cream-edged leaves.

Fuchsias

Fuchsias are equally valuable in the window garden. They can be grown as neat bushy plants by pinching out the top shoots, or as taller pyramids and standards by nipping out side-shoots. The trailing varieties, also, are marvellous at the front of a box.

When grown as tall pyramids or short standards, the fuchsias are, in my view, the best flowers of all for adding height and acting as focal plants in the summer display. Like the pelargoniums, they bloom over a very long period, from mid-summer to late autumn, with quite a variety of flower shape and colour.

The single-flowered varieties are the most elegant, and some of the best are: 'Bon Accord' (lilac and white); 'Brutus' (red and purple); 'Madame Cornelissen' (red and white); 'Mission Bells' (red and purple); 'Rufus the Red' (deep salmon-red) and 'Ting-a-Ling' (pure white).

Good doubles include 'Alice Hoffman' and 'Snowcap' (both red and white); 'Tennessee Waltz' (pink and lilac), and 'Dollar Princess' (red and lilac).

All of the above varieties produce large, rounded flowers, but there are others with long, tubular flowers which dangle in elegant clusters; of these, 'Thalia' is a popular choice for its dark green foliage and orange-red blooms; well worth looking out for.

As for trailing fuchsias, the following are excellent: 'Cascade' (purple-red and white); 'Swingtime' (scarlet and white, double-flowered); and 'Marinka' (red and purple).

Bulbs, tubers, corms

Of the summer-flowering bulbs, tubers and corms, many are too tall for the window garden, but a few are very suitable.

Most popular of all are the tuberous begonias which flower through to autumn. Some of the large-flowered double *Begonia* × *tuberhybrida* varieties are tallish plants which can be used to add height to the display. The dwarfer and smaller-flowered varieties look good as a box edging, and so do the graceful trailing *B.* × *tuberhybrida* 'Pendula' types. The tender tubers can be started into growth indoors in late winter but should not go outside until all danger of spring frost is past. Lift in autumn and store frost-free in dry growing compost.

The poppy-flowered 'De Caen' and the double-flowered 'St Brigid' anemone strains are also popular. For a long season of colour, plant the tubers in small batches from early to late spring.

Freesias specially treated for outdoor summer flowering are offered by bulb growers these days, and their rich fragrance wafting in through an open window is a delight. Plant a handful of corms in spring, and they'll bloom in late summer (earlier if you start them off indoors or under glass in late winter).

Another low-growing summer bulb that I like very much is *Tigridia pavonia* (tiger flower). This is superb at the back of a display where its large and exotic iris-like blooms appear over a long period throughout late summer; usually sold in a mixture of colours ranging from glowing reds, through yellow and mauve to glistening white, all with eye-catching red and purple tiger-markings in the centre.

Most large-flowered gladioli are far too tall for any window garden, but it is possible to use the very smallest hybrids, like the dainty 60 cm (2 ft) *Gladiolus nanus* varieties. Two or three corms planted to sprout up the side of a tall window, for example, would add height and long-lasting colour to the display, and also contribute attractive sword-shaped foliage to contrast with bushier plants. These small varieties would also suit a box slung beneath a window ledge, where taller plants are more easily accommodated without danger of blocking the window too much.

The same comments apply to the sumptuous lilies: most are too tall, but in a low-slung box or as focal plants to the side of a large window, some of the lowest-growing ones would make a stunning feature. For example, there might be a place for a bulb or two of the upright-flowered 'mid-century' hybrids like the popular nasturtium-red 'Enchantment' or the lemon-yellow 'Connecticut King' which grow to between 60 and 90 cm (2 to 3 ft). There are also some very lovely large-flowered and sweetly scented dwarf *Lilium auratum* hybrids coming onto the market. Bred to be grown as sturdy pot plants, these brilliant red and pink flowers are ideal for the window box, where they'll add a truly exotic touch to the whole effect.

Trailers

Now for some attractive trailing foliage plants for the summer window garden: ivies are excellent, of course, plain-leaved varieties providing a dark green foil to set off the colourful flower display, or gold and silver variegated forms for added effect. The silver grey-leaved *Helichrysum petiolatum* is very elegant, providing a good contrast with darker foliage, as does the ferny-leaved silvery-white *Senecio maritimus*.

Various trailing house plants may also be used in the summer window box, including *Chlorophytum comosum* 'Variegatum' (the white variegated spider plant), *Saxifraga stolonifera* (mother of thousands) with its round silver-veined leaves, purple on the undersides, and the stripy-leaved *Zebrina pendula* and tradescantias (wandering Jews).

The most popular bushy plants for bright foliage colour are the flamboyant *Coleus* varieties, instantly recognizable by their nettle-like leaves, strikingly splashed and zoned in all shades of yellow, green, pink, red and maroon-purple. And, of course, in a shady window box ferns are especially useful.

AUTUMN

Most annuals will continue flowering into the autumn, often only stopping when the first frosts arrive; and they'll bloom longer and more generously if the dead flower heads are regularly nipped off, to stop them running to seed. The same goes for most of the tender perennials, particularly the fuchsias, which are especially useful for late colour; but, of course, these tender plants should be removed before frosts threaten, if they're to be kept for the following year.

Bulbs

As autumn advances, however, the display does start to fade. Yet it's a simple matter to revive the window garden by popping in a few autumn-flowering bulbs to provide added colour and interest. These should be planted in late summer or as early as possible in the autumn, and most will spring into growth and start to push up flower buds almost immediately. If they're left unplanted until late autumn, then they tend to start sprouting in the dry state, and the resulting flowers are usually thin, malformed and very disappointing. Rather than risk getting them in this condition from the store or the mail-order company, be sure to buy or order as early as possible.

You can simply poke holes in the growing compost between the summer plants which are still colourful enough to be left, and pop the bulbs in; and any plants that have finished flowering or are starting to look unsightly may of course be removed to make more room.

Be sure to water the window garden heavily after planting bulbs; they'll have to compete with existing plant roots in the box and may flower poorly if the compost is dry. It's also a good idea to give them some liquid fertilizer. By the time the bulbs are up and starting to flower, you'll probably find that more of the summer plants are going over and can be carefully removed to make way for them (cut annuals off at the base, leaving the roots, so as not to disturb the bulbs.)

If you're using pots inside the window box, or removable liners, then of course special displays of autumn bulbs can be planted up and grown on in advance, ready for a quick change-over when the bulbs start to come into flower.

The most spectacular of all the autumn bulbs are the

Text continues on p. 32

Always ensure that hanging baskets are within easy reach for watering and maintenance, particularly when they're to be tended from high windows.

Sweet peas trained on canes clothe this house wall with summer colour; but even so, the effect is greatly enhanced by the addition of a well-stocked hanging basket.

31

colchicums, commonly referred to as 'autumn crocus' although they're actually quite different (except for a basic similarity in flower shape) from the true autumn-flowering crocus. Most of the species and varieties commonly available from stores and mail-order catalogues produce huge goblet-shaped flowers, much larger and showier than true crocus. These emerge leafless from the soil, usually many blooms to a corm, so that even one or two will make an eye-catching display.

You should find *Colchicum byzantinum* and *C.* 'Lilac Wonder' on sale in local stores, and these both produce a long succession of large and very bright lilac-pink flowers, but there are many more to be had from mail-order suppliers, some of them even better than these old favourites. The most flamboyant of all is the large double-flowered pink variety aptly named 'Waterlily'. *Colchicum speciosum* is another beauty, with large tulip-shaped blooms that may be either lilac-rose, deep mauve-red or pure white. The variety 'The Giant' is the largest-flowered, with white-throated violet-pink blooms, and 'Violet Queen' is attractively chequered lilac-pink and deep violet-purple.

As for the true crocus, there are a fair number that bloom in autumn, but probably the best of all is the large-flowered *Crocus speciosus*. Various colour forms are available from good bulb catalogues, all shades of lilac-blue, sometimes very close to a true sky-blue, a wonderful sight when even a handful of corms are clumped together. There's also a stunning white form. Like the colchicums, *C. speciosus* produces a succession of many flowers from each corm over a fairly long period. Other autumn crocus to look out for in the catalogues include the violet-flowered *C. medius* and the rosy-lilac *C. kotschyanus* (formerly *C. zonatus*).

Autumn-flowering hardy cyclamen are the other main standby for this time of year, and the ever-popular *Cyclamen hederifolium* (formerly *C. neapolitanum*) is lovely in a window garden where its small nodding pink flowers can be admired at close quarters; and keep an eye out for the equally beautiful white form, *C. hederifolium album*.

Finally, a bulb or two of the hardy *Nerine bowdenii* would enhance any autumn window garden, with its large clusters of bright pink funnel-shaped flowers.

Naturally, all of these need to grow on after flowering, during the winter and the following spring, if they're to bloom again in the future. With pots or removable liners, this is no problem; they can simply be removed to make way for winter and spring flowers. If they're planted direct into the window box, they'll have to be carefully lifted and either planted out in the garden or potted up, so as not to hinder further seasonal plantings.

WINTER

This is the most difficult season in the window garden, as it is in gardening generally. In areas with a very mild climate, tender perennials and annuals can be had in flower almost the whole year round; but in most areas you have to rely on dwarf winter-flowering bulbs and a few neat winter-flowering perennials, dwarf shrubby plants and evergreens for attractive foliage.

Evergreen perennials and dwarf shrubs are best used for permanent displays, since they resent frequent disturbance and replanting. However, if you're using pots or removable liners in the window box then you can, of course, introduce this kind of winter display quite easily; simply have these plants growing on in pots or liners, ready for the seasonal change over.

If planting direct into a window box full of compost (without a removable liner) one or two pot-grown perennials or dwarf shrubs may be plunged in the growing medium to bulk out the winter show.

These kinds of 'permanent' plants will be discussed in more detail later. For now, here are a few suggestions that are particularly useful for incorporating into the winter window garden, either for flower or evergreen foliage effect (see later comments and plant lists for details). *Erica carnea* and *E.* × *darleyensis* varieties (winter-flowering heathers); dwarf conifers (for added height, shape and foliage colour); ivies (plain-leaved and variegated); colourful-leaved sempervivums (houseleeks) and sedums (stonecrops); the shrubby

Euonymus fortunei 'Silver Queen' (creamy-white variegated leaves); and *Carex morrowii* 'Evergold' (a neat evergreen golden-leaved grass).

Bulbs and corms

Apart from these, however, much can be done to brighten up the winter window garden with a few small bulbs and perhaps some tough winter-flowering pansies. The bulbs – and the pansies, and also any of the temporary perennial plants for winter listed above – should be planted in autumn, of course, somewhat later than the autumn-flowering bulbs. Using pots and removable window box liners, they can follow on from the autumn bulbs. Growing direct in the box, they'll have to be planted amongst the autumn bulbs as these start to sprout and flower; and at this time more summer plants may be removed to create further free space.

The hardy *Cyclamen coum* is superb, often pushing up the first of its dainty, nodding ruby-red or carmine-pink blooms in time for Christmas or the New Year, and continuing in flower for months. The glossy green or silver-zoned leaves are also very pleasing to the eye.

Snowdrops look good with the winter-flowering cyclamen. *Galanthus elwesii* is a particularly large and early-flowering species (often double the size of the ordinary snowdrop); you'll find this in the better bulb catalogues, or sometimes in stores and markets offered as 'large single snowdrops'. *G. nivalis* (common snowdrop) is easily obtained from local stores, and mixing single-flowered bulbs with the doubles adds variety and creates a very attractive effect.

If you're going to plant snowdrops with *Cyclamen coum,* then complete the picture with the golden buttercup-flowered *Eranthis hyemalis* (winter aconite); all should flower together and make a real picture.

The dwarf bulbous irises are also marvellous for winter colour, and particularly for adding a touch of brilliant blue to the display. *Iris reticulata* in its various colour forms is the most popular choice. The bulbs sold in stores and markets are usually either the ordinary deep purple-blue, or mixed colours ranging from purple-red to pale blue. Better still, order named varieties from the better bulb catalogues, since bold clumps of the same colour always look better than the 'bitty' effect produced by a mixture. The varieties 'Harmony' and 'Joyce' are two of the best, both large-flowered deep sky-blues with contrasting orange and yellow crests to the falls; 'Cantab' is a delightful clear pale china-blue; 'Clairette' is an eye-catching bicolour, pale blue with darker blue falls; 'J.S. Dijt' is sweetly scented and a rich red-purple; and 'Violet Beauty' is a large-flowered deep violet-blue.

Striking as the *I. reticulata* varieties are, *I. histrioides* 'Major' is my all-time favourite. The flowers are larger and more robust than any of the above, standing up to winter weather well, and they're the clearest sky-blue imaginable. For contrast with all these blues, try the bright lemon-yellow *I. danfordiae*.

Some of the early-flowering dwarf rock garden narcissi are also excellent for a splash of yellow in the winter window box; try the golden *Narcissus bulbocodium* (hoop petticoat daffodil) which should flower around the same time as the cyclamen, irises, snowdrops, etc.

If you fancy some very early-flowering crocus, look out for the dainty lilac-blue species *Crocus laevigatus* 'Fontenayi' in specialist bulb catalogues; like the cyclamen, it starts doing its thing as early as Christmas and the New Year. The numerous varieties of *C. chrysanthus* start their display in late winter; 'Blue Pearl', 'Cream Beauty', 'E.A. Bowles' (butter-yellow) and 'Snowbunting' (white) are some of the best. These produce many flowers to a corm, so even a small clump makes an eye-catching show, and they continue in colour right through to spring.

Of course, there are many more dwarf bulbs ideal for the window garden, and some of these bloom from late winter to spring, while others join the larger bulbs in boosting the main spring display. Indeed, it's difficult to tell when late winter ends and spring begins where bulbs are concerned, but the rest of the dwarf rock garden type species and varieties will probably be better listed under spring flowers.

Text continues on p. 36

Hanging basket plants trail downwards and mingle attractively with border plants below: note the choice of red flowers to contrast with the whitewashed wall; while paler blooms stand out well in the shade, against the green of the conifer.

Classic hanging basket plantings: tall fuchsias and pelargoniums in the centre, circled with bushier plants, and trailing lobelias planted through the sides of each basket.

Pansy

To end the winter planting suggestions, that popular old bedding favourite, the pansy must be mentioned. Most strains and varieties bloom from spring onwards (and more on these later) but even more useful are the winter-flowering types. They can be raised from seed sown in spring or early summer, to be planted out when they start to bloom in late autumn, and they should continue right through the winter to spring. Usually they are sold as selected red, yellow, violet-blue and white seed strains, or mixed. Alternatively, buy ready-grown plants in autumn from stores or markets.

SPRING

This can be almost as colourful a season as summer, using a combination of bulbs chosen for a succession of flowers from one month to the next, plus a selection of early-flowering bedding plants (Fig. 10).

Once again, as in the other seasons, growing plants and bulbs in removable liners or pots allows more flexibility. Displays of dwarf spring bulbs, daffodils and tulips may be grown on to replace the winter display; or set-pieces can be planned, like daffodils and primroses for early colour, followed by a show of later-flowering tulips.

Where pots or liners are not used, the larger spring bulbs will have to go into the window box with the dwarf winter-flowering bulbs in autumn, to provide a succession of colour from winter through to spring.

Ideally, the spring bedding plants (e.g. primroses and polyanthus) should also go into the box in autumn. However, you can always pick up a few of these from the market or store in spring, and pop them in for a quick boost to the display.

Bulbs

Virtually all spring bulbs are suitable for window gardens, but where daffodils and tulips are concerned, the smaller species and varieties are best; they stand up to

Fig. 10. Spring bulbs and bedding plants arranged into a classic window garden layout, using *Narcissus* 'February Gold', primroses and polyanthus, pansies, forget-me-not, *Narcissus* 'Baby Moon', crocus and *Tulipa praestans* 'Fusilier'.

wind and weather better, they're short enough for the smallest window display, and you can squeeze more of them in for a greater variety of colour and form.

Of the daffodils, I'd particularly recommend the shorter-growing *Narcissus cyclamineus*, *N. triandrus* and *N. jonquilla* hybrids. The following are especially good: 'February Gold', a shapely little trumpet, very early flowering and one of the best choices; 'Tete-a-Tete', with two dainty yellow trumpets to each stem; 'Jack Snipe', creamy-white with a primrose cup; the elegant triandrus hybrids 'Liberty Bells' and 'Silver Chimes' with their nodding, small-cupped blooms; the highly fragrant *N. jonquilla* (sweet jonquil) and *N. jonquilla* 'Baby Moon'. These are all between 20 and 30 cm tall (8 to 12 in).

As for tulips, the 'rock garden' species and dwarf hybrids are ideal; and my first choice for a truly stunning effect would be the multi-flowered *Tulipa prae-*

stans 'Fusilier'. This little beauty grows to just 23 cm (9 in) but produces a bunch of up to five bright scarlet blooms on each sturdy stem. The following are also excellent, none of them growing to more than 25 cm (10 in): *T. tarda*, white with a yellow centre; *T. kaufmanniana* varieties (waterlily tulips); and the *T. greigii* hybrids with their handsome maroon-red striped leaves.

Hyacinths have also long been popular spring window box flowers, and there's a wide range of colour varieties to choose from these days, from bright pinks and reds, through lavender-blues and mauves to cream and white. They're particularly useful since they bloom over such a very long period.

Of the smaller spring bulbs, the chionodoxas (glory of the snow) and scillas (squills) are invaluable for a welcome touch of blue to offset the dominating yellows and reds of the daffodils and tulips. Spring wouldn't be spring without the crocus, of course. The large-flowered dutch crocus are very bold and bright, but I feel that the smaller species and varieties suit window gardens better. I've already mentioned the chrysanthus varieties as flowers for late winter, but they will continue well into spring. Look out also for *Crocus sieberi* 'Violet Queen'. *C. ancyrensis* ('Golden Bunch'), *C. biflorus* and *C. minimus* in the catalogues.

Other small bulbs suitable for the spring window garden include the blue, white, pink and red forms of *Anemone blanda*, the long-flowering violet-blue *Ipheion uniflorum*, and the blue and white muscaris (grape hyacinths).

Bedding plants

The most popular spring bedding plants, and deservedly so, are the primroses and polyanthus; marvellous for a bright splash of early colour, and the ideal foil to spring bulbs. They bloom over a very long period, helping to fill any gaps in the bulb display, and their lush, fresh foliage hides the bare stems of taller bulbs perfectly.

Although they're perennials, primroses and polyanthus are seldom used as permanent plants in window boxes, since the leaves are unexciting and often rather untidy once flowering is over. But they're wonderful as temporary plants, to be potted up or planted out in the garden for the summer, to be used again the following year. If they've made large clumps, they can be divided up after flowering or in the autumn; this both increases your stocks and keeps them growing and flowering strongly. You can raise them from seed sown in early spring to flower the following year, or buy ready-grown plants in autumn.

Pansies are also popular for spring colour. The winter-flowering types previously discussed will often continue flowering into spring, but you can also buy plants in autumn which have been raised specifically for a spring display. You can raise these and the other popular spring bedding plants from seed yourself, sowing in late spring or early summer to flower the following year, but it's quicker and easier to buy them in ready-grown.

Other suitable spring bedding plants include double-flowered *Bellis* varieties (daisies), dwarf *Cheiranthus* (wallflowers) and *Myosotis alpestris* varieties (forget-me-not).

Naturally, to complete the seasonal window box calendar and come full circle, the spring bedding plants and bulbs must be removed to make way for the summer display. Winter and spring bulbs will still be growing at this time, so these must be either potted up or planted out in a corner of the garden, to finish their growth period before being dried out ready for replanting in autumn; don't dry out the bulbs until the foliage yellows and starts to die back.

SPECIAL EFFECTS

Colour schemes, as I said earlier, are mainly a matter for personal choice and imagination. But there are some classic designs that always look good and are worth mentioning with regard to seasonal planting schemes; particularly those for summer, where there's a wide choice of flower colours to play with.

Single-colour planting schemes can look very classy

indeed. For example, white flowers plus silver and grey foliage plants; such things as *Senecio maritimus* and *Helichrysum petiolatum* for silvery foliage, with white petunias, snow-white sweet peas and white sweet alyssum. All-yellow plantings are also very effective.

Alternatively, groupings of similar colour types work well: like the warm colours, yellows, oranges and red together, contrasted with dark green foliage plants; or cooler tints like blues, mauves, pale pinks and white, with silver and variegated foliage. Blues, whites and silvers always go well together, and grouping pale blue, pink and lilac pastel shades, with a touch of white, also produces a pleasing effect.

Having said all that, I do like a good old cottage-garden mixture of colours as much as any carefully devised scheme. Try both, for variety.

Finally, don't forget what I mentioned in the planning and design chapter about mixing climbers and trailers. You can obtain some lovely effects by planting climbers with different flower colours or foliage tints to twine up through one another. The same goes for different types or colours of trailing plants, where you can place one behind the other so that their foliage and flowers spill out of the box intertwined.

3

PERMANENT PLANTING SCHEMES

Some 'permanent' perennial plants may be used in temporary seasonal planting displays; particularly foliage plants like the ivies. However, the major role for these types of plants is in creating window gardens for a year-round effect without the bother of seasonal replanting. With this kind of display, the only work involved is watering, plus occasional weeding and feeding; with perhaps some periodic cutting-back of any plants that grow too large and threaten to swamp their neighbours.

The main aim with a permanent planting scheme should be to use evergreens for year-round interest; preferably with as wide a variety of leaf shape, growth habit and foliage colour as possible. At the same time, try to include plants to flower in every season, even if you can only squeeze in one for each season. See Fig. 11 for an example of a permanent planting scheme for year-round interest.

All the general design points about aiming for variety of height, growth habit etc, apply particularly to permanent plants. Make a mess of a seasonal planting scheme, and you'll only have to put up with it for a few months before it's due to be replanted anyway; but changing what was intended to be a permanent display requires a conscious effort—an effort that you may not feel like making once planting is complete.

Fig. 11. A permanent window box planted for year-round interest and colour. From *left to right:* variegated ivy trained up canes or trellis, *Armeria maritima,* trailing aubrieta, *Dianthus deltoides,* winter heather (*Erica carnea* var.), *Euonymus fortunei* 'Silver Queen', and trailing *Polygonum vacciniifolium.*

EVERGREENS

Since evergreen foliage plants form the 'backbone' of the permanent window display, let's look at these first.

Ivy

The ivies, *Hedera* species and varieties, really are the most useful; tough, easy and fast growing; suitable for use both as climbers and trailers, either in sun or shade;

and available in a wide range of leaf shape and colour. Being self-attaching, ivies grown as climbers may be planted to cling to the wall beside and around the window. However, most can get very large in time, and it's easier to keep them trimmed and under control if they're growing up canes or a section of trellis (tied in to the support).

You should find a good selection of different types amongst the house-plants on sale in local stores and markets. These can be grown outside, but they should only be planted in late spring or early summer when there's no danger of frost, to give them a chance to get used to outdoor life. The ivies sold as house-plants are the same as the ones sold for the garden; it's just that those kept under cover will have grown soft and therefore need time to adapt and toughen up. Better still, buy ivies that have been grown outdoors specifically for garden use.

Before looking at different types of ivies for foliage interest, this is a good place to refer you back once again to my suggestions in the planning and design chapter about mixing climbers and trailers. Planting two different ivies with contrasting leaves to either twine up one another as climbers or to intertwine as they trail out of the box really can look very good.

In the average window box, small-leaved ivies are most in keeping with the scale of the planting scheme. *Hedera helix* (common ivy) is excellent, offering many varieties with neat foliage; notably 'Adam' (green, edged with white). 'Chicago' (green) and 'Chicago Variegata' (green and cream). 'Bird's Foot' (handsome deeply divided leaves), and 'Silver Queen' (green and silver).

H. helix 'Goldheart' is one of the best yellow-variegated ones, each leaf having a bold central gold zone. Some change colour in winter, like 'Shamrock' and 'Deltoidea' which both become tinged with copper or bronze during the cold months. 'Buttercup' is notable for its bright yellow new leaves, turning pale green as they age. And there are also some dwarf varieties which make tiny bushes, like the cream-mottled 'Little Diamond'.

For variety, however, and especially in spacious window boxes, large-leaved ivies can make an attractive change. The largest of all are the forms of *Hedera canariensis* (Canary Island ivy) and *H. colchica* (Persian ivy); both are available as plain-leaved and variegated plants. 'Hibernica' is a good large-leaved form of the common ivy.

Conifers

Dwarf conifers are superb for adding height to a permanent planting scheme, offering a variety of shape and foliage tints rivalled by few other evergreens. Be sure to choose truly dwarf types, otherwise they'll quickly outgrow the window box. Even some of the slow-growing ones can get quite large after a few years and may have to be removed to the garden, to be replaced with younger specimens.

One of the loveliest is *Juniperus communis* 'Compressa', a tiny spire-shaped juniper which will never outgrow the smallest of window boxes. It puts on no more than 1 cm ($\frac{1}{2}$ in) of growth a year and looks marvellous with low-growing plants and trailers, like the neater rock plants (of which, more later).

Slow-growing forms of *Chamaecyparis lawsoniana* (Lawson's cypress) make similar spire-shaped trees but are much faster growing: the varieties 'Ellwoodii' and 'Ellwood's Gold' will be all right in a decent-sized window box for a few years but will eventually become too large and need to be replaced.

The same comments apply to the prostrate mat-forming conifers. One of these would look good trailing down from a corner of the window garden.

Another of my favourites is the conical Christmas tree-shaped *Picea glauca* 'Albertiana Conica'. This is quite slow-growing, a bright fresh green in colour. Of the more rounded and bushy types, look out for the following: the yellow-tinted *Chamaecyparis lawsoniana* 'Minima Aurea'; the bright blue-grey *Juniperus squamata* 'Blue Star'; *Thuya orientalis* 'Aurea Nana' (green, tipped with yellow); *Abies balsamea* 'Hudsonia' (dark green), and *Cryptomeria japonica* 'Vilmoriniana', a tight bun of tiny foliage which turns bronze in winter (a real little beauty).

Shrubs

Dwarf box trees are also good; clipped to shape, they make an interesting alternative to dwarf conifers and will never grow too large. Try the dwarf hedging box, *Buxus sempervirens* 'Suffruticosa' or the even neater *B. microphylla*.

As for dwarf evergreen shrubs for foliage colour, the small variegated forms of *Euonymus fortunei* are good; particularly the very neat 'Silver Queen', its green leaves edged with bright cream white. 'Emerald and Gold' is still more colourful, tinted pale green, gold and pink. They benefit from spring trimming, to encourage production of new shoots, these showing better colour than old growth.

Heathers

Heathers are marvellous in window boxes, especially the neat-growing winter-flowering types, and their foliage looks good all year round. However, most valuable as far as foliage is concerned are those with golden leaves, like the *Erica carnea* varieties 'Aurea' and 'Foxhollow' (winter and spring flowers); *E. × darleyensis* 'Jack Brummage' (winter-flowering); the *Calluna vulgaris* varieties 'Golden Carpet' and 'Gold Haze' (summer-flowering); and *Erica cinerea* 'Golden Drop' (usually non-flowering, but a fantastic foliage plant).

There are also varieties with silvery grey foliage; *Calluna vulgaris* 'Silver Rose' and 'Silver Queen', for example. But the range of leaf tints is so wide that you. could create an attractive planting scheme using heathers alone; there are all shades of dark greens, pale greens and rich bronze-greens.

The heathers look perfect with dwarf conifers, and you could do a lot worse than stock a window box purely with these two kinds of plant, for a variety of foliage tints all year, plus summer, winter and spring flowers from the different types of heathers.

Remember that the summer-flowering heathers generally need lime-free soil. If you're planting these, be sure to use a lime-free growing compost of the type used for potting rhododendrons and azaleas. The winter-flowering *Erica carnea* and *E. × darleyensis* varieties aren't fussy, and any growing compost will do.

Rock plants

Various other small plants, mainly rock plants, provide evergreen foliage of varying hues. Best of all are the succulent sedums (stonecrops) and sempervivums (houseleeks). These are also useful for their summer flowers, but the main attractions are the grey, red, purple and pink tinted leaves. The *Sedum spathulifolium* varieties are some of the best, like the purple-leaved and golden-flowered 'Purpureum', or the grey rosettes and yellow summer flowers of 'Capablanca'. *Sempervivum arachnoideum* 'Laggeri' is one of the most striking houseleeks, its rosettes covered cobweb-fashion with silvery hairs; and there are numerous others with brightly-coloured fleshy cactus-like rosettes. All are best in a sunny window garden, planted to trail over the front of the box.

Grasses

Dwarf evergreen ornamental grasses can play a part in the year-round window garden as well. I've already mentioned the golden-striped *Carex morrowii* 'Evergold' as something to bulk out the seasonal winter display; but it's just as much at home in a permanent planting scheme. *Festuca glauca* is a bright silvery blue grass which makes small evergreen tufts and looks perfect with heathers; *F. scoparia* is similar, but a beautiful bottle-green.

Ferns

There are one or two hardy evergreen ferns which would be ideal for a window garden in a shady situation; notably, *Polypodium vulgare* (common polypody), especially the dwarf forms; the tiny *Asplenium trichomanes* (maidenhair spleenwort), and the various forms of *Phyllitis scolopendrium* (hart's tongue fern) some of which have wonderful crimped edges to the evergreen fronds.

Text continued on p. 44

Masses of trailing plants here, for a luxuriant 'jungly' effect: silver-leaved *Helichrysum petiolatum*, lobelias, ivy-leaved *Pelargonium peltatum*, and the trailing red-and-white fuchsia 'Cascade'.

42

A well-stocked hanging basket, but note how the white petunias disappear against the whitewashed wall at the top. Try to choose colours to contrast with the background: this situation cries out for more splashes of bright red.

Now for a selection of neat flowering plants and dwarf shrubs: these are arranged according to flowering times, to simplify the choice of plants for colour in different seasons. Virtually all are evergreens with attractive foliage.

SPRING

We're spoiled for choice here, since there are so many neat spring-flowering rock plants that can be used in the window garden, including some excellent trailing plants.

Most popular and colourful are the aubrietas (commonly known, and often mis-spelled, as aubretias). These are spreading, mat-forming plants, easy to grow, ideal for tumbling over the front of a window box, and a solid mass of long-lasting brilliant colour. Mixed seedlings are frequently offered, and you can raise your own from seed; but these are usually disappointing compared with the clear colours of the named red, pink, mauve, blue and purple varieties. Trim them back hard after flowering, to keep them neat and bushy.

Another superb and easily-grown trailer is *Alyssum saxatile*; bright yellow flowers throughout spring, over grey-green foliage. Good varieties include the double-flowered 'Flore Pleno' (a very compact plant) and the silvery leaved, pale primrose yellow flowered 'Citrinum' (also sold as 'Silver Queen'). Cut them back after flowering.

White rock cress, *Arabis caucasica* (also sold as *A. albida*) is another strong grower that's best trimmed hard after flowering; there are white flowers from late winter to early summer.

The stronger-growing rock garden phlox are also ideal, making trailing mats that bloom from late spring to early summer in a range of colours from rose-red, through pink, mauve and lilac to pure white. The strongest growers are the varieties of *Phlox subulata*, like 'Red Wings' (crimson), 'Alexander's Surprise' (deep pink), 'Oakington Blue Eyes' (lilac-blue) and 'White Delight'. Neater and suitable for small window boxes are the pink, mauve and white forms of *P. douglasii*.

Other low-growing plants for spring include the bushy white-flowered *Iberis sempervirens* (perennial candytuft), a tough thing that always does well even in heavily polluted city air; the best variety is the compact-growing 'Little Gem'; *Armeria caespitosa* (dwarf thrift) with pink flowers, and *Primula auricula* varieties (show auriculas).

Small spring-flowering evergreen shrubs suitable for window gardens include the tiniest dwarf rhododendrons and dwarf evergreen azaleas. It's well worth trying these, although they may eventually grow too large for smaller window boxes and, like the conifers, need to be replaced after a few years. They cope well with city air pollution but are best where they're not too exposed to strong winds.

You could also try the tiny, slow-growing evergreen *Berberis stenophylla* 'Corallina Compacta' for its handsome dark green foliage and orange spring flowers; or that very classy dwarf alpine shrub *Daphne retusa*, for its sweetly scented flowers, white tinged with rosy violet.

Dwarf spring bulbs may be used to add extra colour to the spring display; simply push a few bulbs of crocus, snowdrop, *Scilla, Chionodoxa*, dwarf *Narcissus, Iris reticulata*, or whatever, into the growing compost between the plants, or around the edges of the box, in autumn. Carefully scoop them out and dry them off for the summer when the leaves start to die down, taking care not to disturb the plant roots too much.

SUMMER

Dianthus (perennial garden pinks and carnations) are a good choice for summer. Their tight hummocks of grey-green leaves look attractive all year round, especially when contrasted with darker foliage. Modern garden pinks tend to flower over a longer period than the older hybrids, often all summer long; and many are deliciously fragrant. Try both single and double flowered varieties. Some of the stronger rock garden species are also useful, and I'd recommend *Dianthus deltoides* (maiden pink) as a plant to spread and trail over the front of the window box; deep green foliage and small red or deep pink flowers endlessly throughout summer.

Rock garden campanulas are wonderful as trailing plants, cascading their bright blue flowers out of the box. The strongest-growing ones, like *Campanula porscharskyana* and *C. portenschlagiana* will take over the window garden and swamp everything else. Neater ones like *C. garganica,* 'W. H. Paine', and small forms of *C. carpatica* like 'Turbinata' are fine.

Rock garden achilleas are good both for their yellow flowers and their finely-cut grey leaves; try *Achillea tomentosa* and any others that you can find. Some of the alpine saxifrages also have handsome silvery grey foliage, particularly the 'encrusted' types with their lovely leaf rosettes and delicate summer flower plumes.

Armeria maritima (sea thrift) is a nice low, bushy plant with spiky foliage, larger than the dwarf thrift of spring, and in flower for a couple of months. 'Vindictive' is a good rose-pink variety, and for a change there's the white-flowered 'Alba'; both go well with dianthus.

For aromatic evergreen foliage and summer flowers, try the varieties of the common thyme, *Thymus drucei* (previously *T. serpyllum*). There are various named forms, mostly pink or red in flower.

Veronica prostrata (rockery speedwell) in its many named varieties is another favourite strong-growing rock plant that's at home trailing over the edge of a window box; it flowers in early summer, generally blue, but there are pink and white forms as well. This is a vigorous spreader and may need regular trimming back after flowering. The same goes for the popular *Helianthemum* (rock rose). It's an excellent trailing spreader with single yellow, pink, red or white rose-like flowers over a long period; and it's a fast grower which will soon fill out the display, but trim it hard after flowering.

In a lime-free growing compost you could try the stunning sky-blue flowered *Lithospermum diffusum,* a low spreading shrubby plant with true gentian-blue flowers. The varieties usually grown are 'Grace Ward' and 'Heavenly Blue'.

Perfect companions for the blue *Lithospermum* are the golden-flowered dwarf shrubby hypericums. The species *Hypericum olympicum, H. polyphyllum* and *H. reptans* all produce their large yellow blooms from mid-summer to autumn. Also good for a splash of yellow is the low-growing *Oenothera missouriensis* (evening primrose). This, too blooms right through to autumn, with huge canary-yellow flowers. And don't forget the summer-flowering heathers; most bloom for months, continuing into autumn.

AUTUMN

Since there are few small perennials which flower in autumn, the crocus mentioned earlier under seasonal plants for autumn can be used for extra colour at this time of year (*Crocus speciosus, C. kotschyanus* and *C. medius*). Use them as suggested for spring bulbs amongst perennials; pop them in between the permanent plants in late summer, and lift them when they start to die down in late spring or early summer.

Of the neat-growing plants that do bloom at this time, the gentians are noteworthy. *Gentiana septemfida* is an easy one to grow, flowering from late summer into autumn, its blue trumpets carried at the ends of long trailing stems. Rather less easy are the Himalayan autumn gentians. These are some of the loveliest of all, but they need lime-free growing compost and plenty of summer moisture, and they're seldom long-lived. However, the brilliant sky-blue *G. sino-ornata* is the most reliable and well worth trying in a window garden that isn't too hot and sunny (a good companion for ferns, ivies and such-like in a shady window box).

By way of contrast, the low-spreading shrubby *Polygonum vacciniifolium* couldn't be easier to grow, and it will quickly spill over the edge of a window box in a curtain of glossy evergreen leaves. Spikes of rose-red flowers appear from late summer well into the autumn.

Text continues on p. 48

A well thought-out planting: red pelargoniums glow against their whitewashed backdrop, closely matching the paintwork of the door which is also nicely framed with the contrasting silver of the trailing helichrysum.

Lovely effect here; the rich violet–purple flowered *Clematis* 'Jackmanii Superba' trained across the cottage, growing around and framing the hanging basket with its contrasting splash of hotter colours.

A dwarf hardy fuchsia like 'Tom Thumb' or 'Lady Thumb' would also provide late colour well into autumn (as well as flowering freely during late summer), but these small fuchsias are only evergreen in very mild, fairly frost-free regions. In areas subject to severe winter cold they may be killed when grown in a box (although they're reasonably hardy if grown in the garden, the roots will be more exposed to frosts in a box).

One of the neater ground-hugging evergreen cotoneasters might be tried in a large window box, for bright red autumn berries, but would probably need regular clipping back. *Cotoneaster congestus*, the slowest and neatest grower, would be the best bet. Alternatively, in lime-free growing compost, *Vaccinium oxycoccos* (the cranberry) and *V. vitis-idaea* (cowberry or mountain cranberry) could be tried for their attractive red fruits and evergreen foliage.

WINTER

Here again, the permanent display can be given a boost by popping in a few winter-flowering dwarf bulbs in autumn; those types mentioned under seasonal plants for winter are suitable.

Apart from these, we have to rely heavily on attractive evergreen foliage (and especially variegated leaves) plus the bright flowers of the winter heathers, the *Erica carnea* and *E. × darleyensis* varieties. Luckily, these winter heathers bloom over an exceptionally long period, often from late autumn or early winter right through to spring; so you don't need many for a good show, and even one will provide colour for months.

My favourite—apart from the golden-leaved ones already mentioned—is *E. carnea* 'Vivellii', a slow-growing variety with dark bronze and green foliage, and ruby-red flowers. 'Springwood Pink' and 'Springwood White' are excellent, and the pink-flowered 'Darley Dale' and 'Arthur Johnson' are particularly long-flowering, often providing colour from late autumn to winter's end.

THE ROCK GARDEN WINDOW BOX

From these plants lists, it's obvious that rock plants are ideal for window gardens, being low-growing and usually fairly compact. Indeed, it's quite possible to create a complete miniature rock garden, using a dwarf conifer or two and a selection of the neatest rock plants (Fig. 12).

In this case, you needn't be restricted to just the strong-growing rock plants. Most of those suggested so far have been tough, easy things which should thrive even when neglected, but should you make a

Fig. 12. A 'rock garden' window box. Use only one of the very slowest-growing dwarf conifers, such as *Juniperus communis* 'Compressa' shown here. Other plants depicted (*left* to *right*): *Phlox* 'Douglasii', *Armeria caespitosa*, *Saxifraga burserana*, *Gentiana verna*, *Saxifraga cochlearis* and *Dianthus alpinus*.

hobby of rock plants, and are prepared to give them what they need – most importantly, very well-drained gritty growing compost – then you can check out the specialist growers' catalogues and try some of the smaller species and varieties.

A very important point to remember, however, is that the smaller rock plants hate being constantly dripped on during winter. If rain tends to drip heavily onto the window box, tuck your smallest rock plants towards the back, close to the window and away from the drips, or, better still, if you possibly can, choose a window ledge sheltered from prevailing winds and heavy rains.

Of these smaller rock plants, I'd strongly recommend the 'kabschia' saxifrages, the *Saxifraga burserana* forms for example. All make tight little mats or buns of silvery or grey-green foliage studded with almost stemless ruby-red, pink, white or yellow flowers during late winter and early spring. *S. oppositifolia* is similar, but a lovely trailing plant with purple-red or deep pink flowers.

The dainty alpine primulas, too, would look good brightening up a rock garden window box in spring. The lilac-blue forms of *Primula marginata* are superb with their silvery, toothed leaves, and there are some charming little forms of *P. auricula,* the wild parent of the florist's auricula.

Should you concentrate on lots of neat rock plants instead of a few large ones, you could also try the stunning sky-blue spring gentian, *Gentiana verna,* some of the more refined rock garden pinks, like *Dianthus alpinus,* and the dwarf summer-flowering geraniums. Add a rock and one of the tiniest dwarf conifers (e.g. *Juniperus communis* 'Compressa') to complete the picture, plus a top-dressing of grit or fine gravel, and there's your rock garden.

Wide windows, as here, may take two boxes side by side. Note the conifers: dwarf varieties are fine in a window garden for a few years, although most will eventually grow too large and need to be replaced.

Plenty of permanent evergreen foliage interest in this window box: slow-growing conifers and variegated ivies, with one or two temporary bedding plants popped in for summer colour.

4

FRUIT, VEGETABLES AND HERBS

This short chapter will probably be of most interest to those who live in apartments. Where there's no garden to grow fresh fruit and vegetables, and not even a balcony or yard where tubs and pots may be stood, the window box can provide at least one or two vitamin-rich home-grown delicacies for the kitchen.

Office workers might also like to consider planting a box at work with some colourful dwarf tomatoes or some herbs, to liven up those lunch-time sandwiches and add a little extra interest to the working day. A box filled with a selection of culinary herbs outside any kitchen window would be a handy thing from the point of view of a busy cook; simply reach out, snip, and you've a handful of chives or a fresh sprig of parsley to garnish that dish.

Apart from herbs, the best food plants for window gardens include compact-growing things like dwarf bush tomatoes, strawberries (especially the tiny alpine strawberries), and fast-growing small salad vegetables like radish, spring onions and lettuce.

A whole window box may be devoted to these culinary plants, outside the kitchen window for example; either a selection of herbs, a few mixed salad vegetables, a few strawberries, or even a mix of all three in a large box.

Alternatively, if you're in an apartment with only one or two window gardens, then some of these could actually be grown amongst the flowering plants. None of them are ugly, the herbs, dwarf tomatoes and strawberries in particular being quite attractive. If you don't want them to be too obvious from the street, keep them towards the back of the box; in fact, a row of bush tomatoes with their bright red fruits would

make a rather fine backing to a flowering display.

Remember, though, that if they're squeezed into a box with lots of flowering plants, or if they're grown crowded together in a box of their own, then they'll need very regular watering; probably every day in hot weather, and sometimes twice a day. And they'll also need feeding from time to time with liquid fertilizer, especially the fast-growing salad crops.

VEGETABLES

Dwarf bush tomatoes are particularly suited to window-box culture, the fruits ripening well in the warmth reflected from the walls and bathed in reflected sunlight from the window.

There are some excellent very dwarf varieties around now, producing small bite-size tomatoes that are often tastier than larger fruits. You can grow them in pots and slip them into the window box amongst flowering pot plants, but they're better actually planted in a box filled with growing compost. All are easily raised from seed sown on a windowsill indoors in late winter or early spring, and planted out in late spring or early summer when there's no danger of frosts or cold nights to stunt the growth. These tiny tomatoes should need no support under normal conditions, but on a very windy ledge they might be safer tied in to short sticks. Remember to keep them well watered, never allowing them to dry out completely, and feed regularly with liquid fertilizer (special tomato fertilizer is best, but any liquid feed will do).

Radish, lettuce and spring onions may be sown in

the box any time from spring to early summer for summer cropping; the earlier the sowing, the earlier you'll get your salad. All should be kept well watered and fed with liquid fertilizer once a week.

The thinly upright-growing cos lettuce varieties like 'Little Gem' and 'Paris White' are the best space-savers for a window box; or try one of the dwarf butterhead varieties like 'Tom Thumb' which are fast-maturing and produce neat tennis-ball size heads. Better still, grow a loose-leaf variety such as 'Salad Bowl' which produces a mass of curly leaves that can be picked a few at a time without pulling the whole plant; 'Red Salad Bowl' is a novel reddish-brown leaved variety of the same sort that makes an interesting addition to salads.

FRUIT

Of fruits, the only one really suitable for window boxes is the strawberry; and plants grown with their runners trailing over the edge of the box (and cropping on these trailing runners) can look very attractive.

Pot-grown runners may be bought and planted in autumn, to fruit the following summer, but in areas subject to severe winter weather, it's safer to put in young plants in spring, although these won't crop properly until the following year. In regions with extremely low winter temperatures, strawberries are not such a good choice.

Better even than the ordinary garden strawberry are the 'Alpine' varieties like 'Alexandria'. 'Baron Sole-macher' and the golden-fruited 'Yellow Alpine'. These produce small but delicious fruits (perfect for garnishing fruit cocktail and ice cream) which are carried above the plants on elegantly arching wiry stems. They crop all summer long, so there are always a few tasty fruits to pick, and birds don't seem to like them as much as larger varieties, which is an added bonus. The

plants make tidy clumps without runners, and they can be left in the box and cropped year after year. Water and feed frequently in the growing season.

HERBS

Evergreen herbs are very good in a window box, looking attractive and providing garnishes and ingredients for the kitchen all year round (Fig. 13). One of the most popular is thyme, a low-growing twiggy bush with dark evergreen leaves and pretty mauve-pink summer flowers. Common thyme (*Thymus vulgaris*) is the strongest-flavoured. Lemon thyme (*T. x citriodorus*) is milder with a citrus flavour that makes it good for adding to sweet dishes. There are handsome golden-leaved forms of both, excellent for variety of leaf colour and equally useful in the kitchen.

Rosemary is also evergreen and an attractive little shrubby plant with needle-shaped leaves and blue flowers. Regular picking or clipping of the upper shoots will keep it low and tidy, but it will still grow to over 30 cm (1 ft) so place it to one side of the window box.

Fig. 13. A window box Herb garden. Left to right: young bay tree, rosemary (*foreground*), parsley, chives, thyme, (*foreground*) and mint.

Text continues on p. 56

Single-colour plantings can prove just as effective as a rainbow mixture: a selection of all-white flowers with silver foliage plants perhaps, or reds and pinks as in this grouping of pelargoniums.

An exotically-planted urn lends a Mediterranean atmosphere to a town centre frontage where there's only limited space available for a window box display.

Chervil is another tallish evergreen best to one side of the window box, but it can easily be kept to under 30 cm (1 ft) by nipping off the upper leaves regularly. The foliage is very attractive, a fresh green, deeply cut and fern-like.

Parsley will grow throughout the year, but it's best to cut it down in early autumn, to make it produce fresh new leaves for winter, as the old growth becomes tough late in the year; once again, very decorative foliage.

The sweet bay (so good in stews and casseroles) is normally grown as a shrub or small tree, often in a tub sheltered against a sunny wall, but it's fairly slow growing, and a young bush may be grown in a deep window box for some time before it gets too big; regular picking of the leaves and pruning of the shoots will help to keep it small. In severe winters it may be damaged by frost but will often grow away again from the base in spring.

Other herbs to try include chives, marjoram, sage, savory, tarragon, basil and mint. Those that are not evergreen can of course be dried or frozen for winter use. Don't forget about garlic; simply buy a head of garlic from the market, split it up, plant the cloves in early spring and lift fresh juicy bulbs in summer.

These herbs may be planted in a window box filled with growing compost, or they may be grown in pots sitting inside a box, perhaps amongst flowering pot plants. Having them in pots does make it easy to lift them in through the window for picking; and pots of non-evergreen herbs may then be brought inside the window in autumn, to keep them growing into winter for a longer supply of fresh leaves. However, it's not much more trouble to lean out and snip leaves from a herb garden actually growing in a box, and with plenty of evergreens, it'll look good all year.

The exception is mint, which is so strong growing and fast-spreading by underground stems that it will quickly take over the window garden. This should always be grown in a pot. If the rest of herbs are permanent plantings in a box full of compost, then the mint pot may be plunged amongst them, but it should be lifted regularly to remove any underground runners that escape from the pot.

Most herbs may be quickly raised from seed, but it's generally simpler to buy ready-grown plants. Some are annuals (like basil) which must be raised afresh from seed each year (or new plants bought in spring); and some like parsley) are short-lived plants which must also be replaced frequently (although not necessarily every year); but many, including the evergreen shrubby ones, keep going year after year.

5

HANGING BASKETS

It's impossible to discuss window boxes without also mentioning hanging baskets. These look superb one each side of a door, as they're so often used, but they're equally attractive as window decorations. To my eye, hanging baskets complete the picture, draping the window in a cascade of flowers and foliage to complement and balance the box display below, but the placing of them depends greatly on the shape and size of the window.

A narrow window looks best with a single basket fixed above it, and a window which is both narrow and tall simply cries out for this treatment (Fig. 14). The eye is caught by the brimming display in the window-ledge box, and then drawn upwards in a pleasing way to the basket above; the whole forming a classical pyramidal arrangement. Be sure to fix the basket so that it hangs down in front of the top part of the window, so that it may be admired from within as well as from without.

Wider windows call out for a hanging basket on each side, the trailing plants spilling down to almost meet the tall plants and climbers reaching up from the ends of the box below. Indeed, if it can be contrived so that the climbers and tall plants at each end of the window box do actually reach up to mingle with the cascading leaves and flowers of the hanging basket, this 'framing' effect can be truly lovely.

Very large windows might call for a combination of these, with both hanging baskets to each side and one or more baskets above; but take care not to over-do it, or the effect will end up looking cluttered. Better to keep any arrangement of hanging baskets and window boxes fairly simple.

Fig. 14. Fixing a hanging basket over the window, above your box garden, will complete the picture. Where the window is small, site the basket to one side to avoid blocking the light and the view, but make sure you can reach the basket easily for watering purposes etc.

Brackets for hanging baskets may be quickly and easily fitted by any handyman with an electric drill, but do remember that the baskets, once hung, must be within easy reach for watering and other maintenance

Text continues on p. 60

Raised planting troughs brighten a city street: if only more businesses and stores would take the trouble to enliven our dusty towns with flowers and greenery.

A good combination of window boxes and climber: given time and a little training, the climber should frame the displays on these widely-spaced window ledges, linking them into a harmonious whole, and camouflaging the blank expanse of bare wall.

tasks. Baskets by ground-floor windows pose no real problems, but those fixed around upper-storey windows should be easily reached from within the window without any necessity for dangerous leaning out over the ledge. Planting and other maintenance tasks will be discussed later, with window boxes, in a separate chapter. For now, let's look at which plants may be grown in hanging baskets and what effects may be obtained with these.

THE PLANTS

Hanging baskets are only really suitable for summer displays in most regions. Holding only a small volume of growing compost, they're too small for most perennial plants, and they freeze solid and dry out fast in cold winter weather, which does not suit winter and spring flowering bulbs. In mild, fairly frost-free regions, of course, they can provide colour from annuals and tender plants almost the whole year round; but for most of us they are unfortunately a summer phenomenon.

Many of the annuals and tender plants mentioned under temporary plants for summer colour in window boxes are of course suitable for hanging baskets. Very tall plants are obviously not ideal, and the major part of the planting scheme will involve trailing plants.

However, the same rules apply about obtaining a balanced mix of types, and at least one tallish plant should ideally be included, in the centre of the basket, to add height to the display, with trailers planted around it. In a wire basket with open sides, trailers may also be planted to grow out between the wires (see 'Planting and maintenance' chapter).

Pelargoniums and fuchsias are perfect as central 'height' plants in a basket. Hanging baskets tend to be more exposed to wind and rain than window boxes, so any tall plants need to be sturdy; these two suggestions are ideal, whereas tall annuals tend to flop over.

Of trailing plants, the following are all excellent. For foliage: small-leaved ivy varieties, the silvery-leaved *Helichrysum petiolatum* and *Senecio maritimus*, *Saxifraga stolonifera* (mother of thousands) and the stripy-

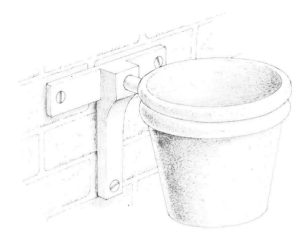

Fig. 15. Brackets to hold pots, fixed to the wall alongside a window, are yet another alternative for brightening up the house; almost as good as hanging baskets.

leaved *Zebrina pendula* (wandering Jew). Flowering plants include trailing begonias (*Begonia×tuberhybrida* 'Pendula' varieties), trailing fuchsias (e.g. 'Cascade', 'Swingtime' and 'Marinka'), the ivy-leaved *Pelargonium peltatum* varieties, *Lobelia erinus* 'Pendula' varieties (e.g. 'Blue Cascade' and 'Red Cascade'), petunias (e.g. the pink 'Blush Cascade' and the red 'Ruby Cascade'), *Lysimachia nummularia* (creeping Jenny), *impatiens* (busy Lizzie) and *Tropaeolum majus* (nasturtium). For hanging baskets in shade, the following are the best choices: *Lysimachia nummularia* (and its golden-leaved form 'Aurea'), the ivies, *Saxifraga stolonifera*, *Zebrina pendula*, lobelias, nasturtiums, trailing fuchsias and begonias.

Finally, if hanging baskets seem like too much trouble, how about fixing wall-mounted pot holders (Fig. 15)? These are almost as attractive, spilling over with colourful trailing plants. If possible, try to get ones that will hold a largish pot with more than one plant; say a trailer plus a bushy plant; and small wall-mounted 'planters' (small plastic troughs or semi-circular containers) fixed with brackets, one each side of the window, provide yet another interesting alternative.

6

PLANTING AND MAINTENANCE

As in any form of gardening, the more care you take over planting, watering, feeding and so forth, the better the end result will be. The most carefully thought-out planting schemes are so easily spoiled by careless planting and indifferent maintenance; which, in the end means wasted time and effort. Annuals in particular need good quality growing compost plus regular watering and feeding if they're to grow fast, come into flower early and make a superb display.

GROWING COMPOSTS

Never use unsterilized garden soil in containers; the chances are that it will contain soil pests, weed seeds and plant disease spores which can cause havoc in the confines of a pot or window box. The average garden soil is, in any case, often far from perfect as a growing medium. It may be too heavy and sticky or very sandy and dry, or short on essential plant foods and trace elements necessary for healthy growth.

You can make up your own growing compost by sterilizing garden soil, adding peat and fertilizers, but that's a long and tiresome process. Better to buy bags of commercially-produced composts which are guaranteed pest and disease free, with a correct balance of ingredients to ensure strong growth.

Soilless peat-based potting compost is best for fast-growing temporary plants like annuals, tender perennials, spring bedding plants and bulbs; the plants can root into it quickly, and it's light and easy to work in when it comes to regular seasonal planting, lifting and replanting.

There's no need to replace the compost every time you replant for a new season; it'll do for the whole year with just a little topping up as necessary when you replant. Once it has been used to grow your summer, autumn, winter and spring displays, it will be exhausted and in poor condition; so use the old compost as a soil improving material in the garden, and start again with fresh potting compost.

Soil-based potting compost is better for permanent plants (including perennial herbs). It stays in good condition for much longer and retains plant foods better, so your permanent planting display can be left undisturbed for quite a few years.

Should you wish to grow the smaller, more 'special' alpines in a 'rock garden box' as described earlier, then these should be given a particularly well-drained, gritty soil. Mixing three measures of soil-based potting compost with one measure of horticultural grit or fine gravel (measured by bulk) is ideal. Don't forget to top-dress with a layer of grit or gravel, tucking this under the leaves of the tiny rock plants to help keep their necks dry and prevent rain splashing soil onto the delicate flowers.

DRAINAGE

It's essential that any window box should have holes in the base for drainage of excess water, to prevent the growing compost becoming waterlogged and going sour. Roots simply cannot grow in waterlogged soil, and where drainage is poor or even non-existent, the plants are liable to die very quickly, especially if

Text continues on p. 64

In a shady situation like this basement, shade-loving impatiens varieties (busy lizzies) thrive.

More town houses with this kind of summer floral display would be a welcome sight on our streets.

waterlogging occurs during winter. This applies particularly to boxes filled with compost, but also to boxes intended to hold pots or removable liners; water collecting around the pots or liners will make the compost in them equally wet and sour.

Make sure that the drainage holes are reasonably large and that there are enough of them – four or five in a medium-sized box; more in a very large container. To ensure that they won't become blocked by the growing compost, place a small pile of broken flower-pot pieces, broken bricks or small stones over each hole. The box may then be filled with growing compost, taking care not to disturb the drainage material. Better still, to ensure perfect drainage, cover the holes as suggested, then also cover the base of the box with a 2-cm (1-in) layer of gravel or grit, the compost going in on top of this drainage layer; this is particularly advisable for permanent plantings, to ensure good long-term drainage.

If you're planning to grow the tiniest rock plants in a specialized rock garden window box, use a gritty compost mixture as mentioned earlier, but also put an extra-deep layer of drainage grit or gravel in the base; preferably 4 to 5 cm (1½ to 2 in).

PLANTING

Your plants should not be crammed into the box so close together that there's no room for root growth. Make sure that there's some compost between the rootballs for them to grow out into, but don't space them out too much; you want their top-growth to mingle together in a luxuriant mass of flowers and foliage.

Always water the plants (in their pots or trays) before planting them, to be sure that their rootballs are moist; never plant anything with dry roots. Water thoroughly after planting; a really good soaking until water seeps out of the drainage holes. Don't over-fill the box with compost. The surface of the compost should be about 2.5 cm (1 in) below the rim of the container, to catch and hold water.

When mixing bulbs with bedding plants (for a winter or spring display) always put the plants in first, then pop the bulbs in around them; do it the other way around, and you may damage the bulbs with the trowel when you put the plants in later. Use your hands for planting, of course, and this problem doesn't arise.

Remember that the larger the bulb, the deeper it should be. Dwarf bulbs need only have their tips about 2.5 cm (1 in) below the surface, but larger daffodils and tulips should have more like 5 to 8 cm (2 to 3 in) of compost over their tips, preferably more. Much depends on the depth of the box, though; don't put large bulbs so deep that their bases sit almost at the bottom of the container.

If you're using climbers that need support from canes or trellis, put the support in first, and then the plant, to avoid spearing and damaging roots. Tie the climbers in to the supports gently with soft twine, not too tightly so that their stems may grow and expand.

On a general point, don't forget the design suggestions made in my first chapter. Do go for a variety of plant types, with tall focal plants or climbers to the sides of the box, grading down to smaller, bushier things in the centre, and trailers towards the front. Don't start planting straight away, either. Stand back and imagine the effect you're aiming for, double-checking that everything is going in its right place. If the plants are pot-grown, try placing them on the surface of the compost, arranging and re-arranging them until you're happy with the layout.

WATERING

Try not to let the window box dry out completely at any time, and particularly when young plants are growing fast before flowering.

Never wait for plants to start wilting before you bother to water. If they're short of water, they'll stop growing and suffer a setback long before wilting becomes obvious; and they can then take some time to recover, so that flowering may be delayed.

In hot weather you'll probably find that a well-stocked window box in a sunny position may need watering once a day or perhaps even twice a day. Watering in the mornings and evenings is best, and you should always avoid splashing the plants' foliage in sunny summer weather; water droplets on leaves act like magnifying glasses, concentrating the sun's rays and scorching the plants.

However, too much water can be as bad as none at all. Test the compost with your finger to see if it's drying out below; if so, fill the box to the rim with the watering can. Do not water again until the compost once more starts to feel just barely moist. The ideal is to keep it damp but not soaking wet. Watering should be minimal in winter, just enough to stop the growing compost drying out, and it may not be required at all. Small rock plants in particular need hardly any watering at this time of year.

FEEDING

Seasonal plants will need more feeding than a permanent planting display, since things like annuals, tender perennials and bulbs grow fast and quickly exhaust the soil. Peat-based composts used for seasonal plants also tend to lose their plant foods quickly, these being easily washed out by rain and watering. Peat composts will feed the plants adequately for a few weeks after first being planted, but after that, you should water with liquid fertilizer every two or three weeks during summer. Feed winter and spring seasonal plants including bulbs) less frequently, say once immediately after planting and once or twice in the spring.

The best liquid fertilizers to use are those with a high-potash content, which encourages flowering rather than excessive foliage growth (tomato fertilizer is suitable, being very high in potash). Liquid feeds which also contain trace elements are particularly good, preventing deficiencies of these essential minerals.

Permanent plantings require less heavy feeding. For one thing, the soil-based composts in which they're usually grown hold plant nutrients longer; secondly

you don't want the plants to grow too vigorously or they may quickly become too large for the box; and thirdly, most of the smaller flowering perennials generally bloom more freely when not over-fed. One dose of a high-potash liquid fertilizer in the spring should do (with a second dose in summer only if the plants look like they really need a boost).

If the growing compost is dry, give your plants some water before feeding with liquid fertilizer; applied to dry compost, it may harm the roots, and never make the mixture stronger than recommended on the bottle.

HANGING BASKETS

Wire baskets should be lined with moss (available from garden stores) and filled with a peat-based potting compost. One or two trailing plants may be inserted in the sides, to grow out through the wire and moss. Place these in position as you line and fill the basket. Finally, plant the top with more trailers and some taller and bushier things (Fig. 16). Bring the moss right to the brim of the basket, but the compost level should be below this, to allow for watering. After planting, give the basket a good soaking and keep it out of the sun for a couple of days, if possible, to let the plants settle in before hanging.

Baskets do dry out fast and may need watering once or even twice a day in hot weather. The most effective way to water is to take the basket down and dunk it in a bowl of water until the compost is soaked through. In very hot weather, it's best to do this at least once or twice a week, in addition to a daily sprinkling with the watering can. Feed with liquid fertilizer every two or three weeks.

If you're unable to carry out such frequent watering in summer, put a lining of polythene inside the moss to help conserve the moisture. But be sure to punch some holes in the base of the polythene to allow for drainage of excess water; and make slits in the sides to allow you to plant trailers. Placing a saucer on the moss lining in the base, before filling with compost, also helps to

Text continues on p. 68

Here, in the absence of a ledge, the owner has used brackets to support a box below the window. This also allows taller plants to be used in the display.

Imaginative use of the ledges over bay windows transforms this frontage in summer. Always make sure that window boxes and pots on a street front are well secured.

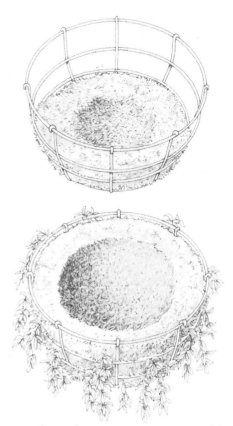

Fig. 16. (*a*)–(*c*) Making up a hanging basket. First place a pad of sphagnum moss in the bottom of the basket, then place a handful or two of compost on the moss and push two or three trailing plants through the wires. Repeat the process with another series of plants; bushy plants can be placed in the top.

prevent water from draining away too quickly, and to hold a small reserve of moisture for the roots.

Solid plastic hanging plant containers require less frequent watering (although they'll still dry out quite fast) but then you can't plant trailers in the sides of these; and I do like the attractive moss-lined effect of the traditional open basket.

GENERAL CARE

One of the most important periodic tasks is to nip off dead flower heads, to prevent energy being wasted on seed production and to encourage prolonged flowering instead.

Often, trimming a plant with shears or scissors after it finishes flowering will induce it to produce a second flush of colour. This is worth trying with all plants that make strong, straggly growth, although not all will respond. Trimming is to be recommended in any case for the strongest-growing perennials like aubrietas, arabis, *Alyssum saxatile,* campanulas, helianthemums and *Iberis sempervirens* (candytuft). Cutting back the spent flowering shoots keeps them neat as well as ensuring good flowering the following year, and quite possibly some extra flowers the same year. Try this with annuals, too.

Weeding is the only other regular task. In the crowded conditions of a window box or hanging basket, added competition for root space, water and food is the last thing your plants need, so get any weeds out as soon as you spot them, and before they become large enough to provide serious root competition.

7

PROBLEMS WITH YOUR PLANTS

Give your window garden plants good quality growing compost, water them regularly (not too much, not too little), feed as suggested earlier, and you should have few real problems. Healthy, well-grown plants will be better able to survive unseen disasters like insect or disease attack, scorching hot weather, frosts and other gardening plagues. Poorly grown plants, on the other hand, will often give up the fight at the first sign of any trouble.

To fully describe and discuss all the diseases, pests and cultural disorders that can strike plants down would fill a book in itself. Let's look briefly, however, at some of the most common troubles that might crop up.

GROWING PROBLEMS

Stunted growth, wilting, brown-scorched leaves and dying shoots may be due to various causes, but look first to the growing conditions. These symptoms are classic signs of drought, but they can also be due to waterlogged soil causing the roots to rot. Always check the growing compost first to see whether it's either too dry or too wet (both conditions are equally serious).

Plants which have suffered drought damage in hot weather will revive more quickly if they're given some shade and shelter from the wind in addition to watering. Pop plant pots over them, or pin shading material (netting or even sheets of newspaper) over the entire window box for a day or two after watering.

Frost damage, when severe, shows on tender plants and young annuals as a blackening and shrivelling of soft shoots and leaves. Mild frost damage may appear only as a yellowing of the leaves, and the plants will recover. Even hardy plants used in permanent displays may be damaged by severe frosts, this usually showing as a browning of the leaves. Where frost damage is bad, cut out all affected shoots to prevent rot setting in, and hope that new growth will appear. Annuals and tender plants killed to soil level will seldom recover and should be replaced.

If sharp frosts are forecast after you've planted tender things, protect them by pinning sheets of newspaper over the box as insulation. Always check that any annuals and bedding plants you buy in have been 'hardened off'; that is, they've been grown under cold conditions outside or in cold frames for a while, to acclimatize them to outdoor life and toughen them up.

PESTS

Birds may sometimes damage window box plants, pulling out seedlings, pecking leaves and tearing at flowers (especially in spring). If this happens, tie some strands of black sewing cotton between small sticks, criss-crossing the window box. Only two or three strands towards the front will be needed and shouldn't look too unsightly. This will keep the birds off without harming them, and it can be removed after a week or so when the birds have given up and gone elsewhere.

Aphids are the commonest and most serious insect pests, crippling plants by sucking sap from young

Text continues on p. 72

A lovely traditional 'cottagey' mixture with lots of hot reds and warm pinks.

Boxes on high ledges, like hanging baskets, are mainly admired from below; so a predominance of colourful trailing plants, as here, is an excellent idea.

leaves and shoot-tips, and also sometimes infecting plants with serious virus diseases. Watch out for infestations on new growth, particularly in late spring and early summer, and spray immediately with malathion or (better still) a long-lasting systemic insecticide.

Slugs and snails may find their way up walls into window gardens, particularly in wet seasons. If they become a problem, scatter some slug-killer pellets into the box, underneath the foliage of the plants where these creatures hide.

Other insect pests are too numerous to list, but symptoms such as pale yellow-mottled leaves, notches eaten out of leaves, white 'tunnels' burrowed through leaves and twisted, malformed foliage often indicate insect activity. If serious symptoms appear, the best thing to do is to spray with a systemic insecticide recommended for dealing with a wide range of different pests (your local gardening store will advise on available brands).

DISEASES

Grey mould (botrytis) is one of the commonest diseases affecting the kinds of seasonal plants and bulbs used in window boxes, particularly where these are grown in crowded conditions, and most frequently in damp weather. It shows as a furry grey growth on soft shoots and leaves, which eventually rot and collapse. On many plants, and especially on bulbs, this starts low down, at or near soil level. It can be halted by spraying with a fungicide containing benomyl.

Other typical signs of plant disease include mouldy, sooty grey or powdery white coatings on leaves and stems; sudden wilting despite the compost being neither too dry nor too wet; and brown spotting of leaves. The simplest thing, if symptoms like these appear, is to spray with a systemic fungicide that deals with a wide range of diseases (once again, local stores will advise on brands).

Finally, any plant which has suffered a setback from poor growing conditions, weather damage, insect or disease attack, may be given a quick boost towards recovery by foliar feeding. This 'shot in the arm' treatment is great for any plant that isn't doing well, the foliar fertilizer being sprayed onto the leaves and absorbed straight into the plant tissues.

Do not spray insecticides, fungicides or foliar fertilizers onto plants in hot sun, otherwise scorch damage may occur. In hot weather, it is better to wait for lower temperatures in the evening.

APPENDIX: PLANT LISTS

Note: (HB)=suitable for hanging baskets

SEASONAL PLANTS

Summer

FOLIAGE PLANTS

Chlorophytum comosum 'Variegatum' (spider plant); tender perennial trailer; leaves striped white and green. (HB)

Coleus varieties; tender bushy perennials; leaves zoned in bright shades of red, pink, purple, green and yellow.

Ferns; both hardy outdoor types and tender pot-plant types may be used; good choice for very shady window boxes.

Hedera species and varieties (ivies); hardy perennial climbers and trailers; plain green, silver and gold variegated. (HB)

Helichrysum petiolatum; frost-tender perennial trailer; silver-grey. (HB)

Saxifraga stolonifera (mother of thousands); tender perennial trailer; silver-veined leaves. (HB)

Senecio maritimus; bushy half-hardy annual; deeply cut foliage, silvery-white. (HB)

Zebrina pendula (wandering Jew); tender perennial trailer; leaves striped cream and green. (HB)

FLOWERING TRAILERS

Alyssum maritimum (sweet alyssum); hardy annual; white or lilac flowers; 'Tiny Tim' and 'Snowcloth' are low, trailing white varieties.

Begonia×tuberhybrida 'Pendula'; tender tuberous-rooted perennial; 'Golden Shower', 'Red Cascade' and 'Pink Cascade' are good. (HB)

Fuchsia; tender perennial; usually red-and-purple or red-and-white; 'Cascade', 'Swingtime' and 'Marinka' are good trailing varieties. (HB)

Impatiens (busy Lizzie); tender perennial usually treated as half-hardy annual; pink, red, mauve and white; the 'Futura' varieties are the best trailers. (HB)

Lathyrus odoratus (sweet pea); hardy annual; although usually treated as a climber, will also make a good trailer. (HB)

Lobelia erinus 'Pendula' varieties; half-hardy annual; e.g. 'Red Cascade'. 'Sapphire' (deep blue) and 'Cascade Mixed' (red, blue, pink, lilac and white). (HB)

Pelargonium peltatum (pendulous geranium); tender perennial; ivy-shaped leaves, red, pink or mauve flowers; also variegated-leaved, white flowered variety 'L'Elegante'. (HB)

Petunia; half-hardy annual; pink, red, lilac, mauve, purple and white; choose trailing varieties like 'Blush Cascade' (pink) and 'Ruby Cascade'. (HB)

Thunbergia alata (black-eyed Susan); half-hardy annual; black eyed yellow or orange flowers; a climber that also looks good when allowed to trail. (HB)

Tropaeolum majus (nasturtium); hardy annual; yellow, orange or red; best trailing varieties include 'Golden Gleam', 'Orange Gleam' and 'Scarlet Gleam', all semi-double. (HB)

BUSHY FLOWERING PLANTS

Ageratum houstonianum (floss flower); half-hardy annual; fluffy blue, pink or white flower, 15–25 cm (6–10 in) according to variety.

Alyssum maritimum (sweet alyssum); hardy annual; white or lilac, 8–15 cm (3–6 in); both bushy and trailing varieties available. (HB)

Anchusa capensis 'Blue Angel'; hardy annual; blue flowers, 23 cm (9 in).

APPENDIX: PLANT LISTS

Antirrhinum majus (snapdragon); half-hardy annual; yellow, orange, red or pink, dwarf varieties 15–20 cm (6–9 in).

Begonia semperflorens (fibrous-rooted begonia); tender perennial, usually treated as half-hardy annual; red, pink or white, often with bronze-tinted foliage, 15–30 cm (6–12 in) according to variety. (HB)

Begonia×tuberhybrida (tuberous begonia); tender tuberous perennial; large double rose-like blooms, red, orange, yellow, pink and white, 25–45 cm (10–18 in). (HB)

Calceolaria (slipper flower); half-hardy annual; yellow, orange or red, 15–30 cm (6–12 in).

Dahlia (dwarf bedding varieties); tender tuberous perennials, usually treated as half-hardy annuals; single or double flowers, red, yellow, orange, pink or white, 30–60 cm (1–2 ft).

Dimorphotheca aurantiaca (star of the veldt); hardy annual; yellow, orange, pink and white daisy flowers, 30 cm (1 ft).

Eschscholzia (Californian poppy); hardy annual; orange, red and yellow poppy flowers, 15–30 cm (6–12 in).

Fuchsia; tender perennial; elegantly dangling red, white, red-and-purple or red-and-white flowers; height depends on training, generally 30–60 cm (1–2 ft). (HB)

Gazania; half-hardy annual; yellow, orange and red daisy-like flowers, 23–30 cm (9–12 in).

Godetia grandiflora; hardy annual; large funnel-flowers, crimson, pink, mauve and white, 23–38 cm (9–15 in).

Iberis umbellata (candytuft); hardy annual; fragrant white, pink or red flowers, 23–38 cm (9–15 in).

Impatiens (busy Lizzie); tender perennial usually treated as half-hardy annual; pink, red, mauve and white, 15–30 cm (6–12 in). (HB)

Limnanthes douglasii (poached egg flower); hardy annual; white blooms with egg-yolk-yellow centre, and ferny foliage, 15 cm (6 in).

Lobelia erinus; half-hardy annual; red, blue, pink, violet and white, 10–20 cm (4–8 in). (HB)

Malcolmia maritima (Virginia stock); hardy annual; strongly scented, white, mauve, pink and red, 15–20 cm (6–8 in).

Mesembryanthemum (Livingstone daisy); half-hardy annual; white, pink, red, orange and yellow daisy flowers, 10 cm (4 in).

Mimulus (monkey flower); half-hardy annual; red, orange and yellow trumpet-flowers, 15–30 cm (6–12 in). (HB)

Nemesia strumosa; half-hardy annual; red, cream and yellow, 23–30 cm (9–12 in).

Nemophila menziesii (baby blue eyes, Californian bluebell); white-centred sky-blue flowers, 15 cm (6 in).

Nicotiana alata (tobacco plant); half-hardy annual; various colours, 30–60 cm (1–2 ft).

Pelargonium (geranium); tender perennial; handsome leaves and red, pink, lilac or white flowers, 20–45 cm (8–18 in) according to variety. (HB)

Petunia; half-hardy annual; large funnel-shaped flowers (doubles and singles), red, pink, mauve, lilac, blue and white, 15–30 cm (6–12 in). (HB)

Phlox drummondii; half-hardy annual; many colours, 15–30 cm (6–12 in).

Salvia splendens; half-hardy annual; dark green leaves and large spikes of bright red flowers, 23–45 cm (9–18 in).

Tagetes (dwarf French marigolds); double and single yellow, orange and red marigold flowers, 15–30 cm (6–12 in).

Viola (pansy); various colours, 15–23 cm (6–9 in). (HB)

Zinnia; half-hardy annual; large daisy-like flowers, single or double, wide range of colours, 15–60 cm (6–24 in) according to variety.

CLIMBERS

Cobaea scandens (cathedral bells); half-hardy annual; large purple-blue bell flowers.

Eccremocarpus scaber (Chilean glory flower); half-hardy annual; orange tubular flowers.

Hedera (ivies); hardy perennials; see foliage plants.

Ipomoea (morning glory); half-hardy annual; 'Heavenly Blue' is the most popular variety, a deep sky-blue flower.

Lathyrus odoratus (sweet pea); popular hardy annual; needs no description from me, but look out for the strongly-scented 'old-fashioned' strains.

Thunbergia alata (black-eyed Susan); half-hardy annual; black-eyed orange, yellow or creamy-white flowers.

Tropaeolum majus (nasturtium); hardy annual; the climbing varieties are as easy to grow as the bushy trailing nasturtiums; red or yellow flowers.

BULBS, CORMS AND TUBERS

Anemone 'de Caen'; hardy tuber; single poppy flowers, red, pink, mauve, blue and white, 15–25 cm (6–10 in).

Anemone 'St. Brigid'; hardy tuber; double flowers, same colour range and height as above.

Freesia; tender corm; specially treated corms for outdoor summer flowering available from catalogues; normally sold as mixtures of yellow, red, violet and lilac-blue.

Gladioli; tender corm; short-growing types, like the 'Nanus' hybrids, white, pink and rose-red, up to 60 cm (2 ft).

Lilium (lilies); hardy bulbs; short-growing hybrids like 'Enchantment' (nasturtium-red) and 'Connecticut King' (yellow), 60–90 cm (2–3 ft).

Autumn

Colchicum (often incorrectly called autumn crocus); hardy corm; large lilac-pink, mauve-pink, rosy-purple and white goblet-shaped flowers (like giant crocus), 15–20 cm (6–8 in).

Crocus kotschyanus (*C. zonatus*); hardy corm; lilac-pink, 10 cm (4 in).

C. medius; hardy corm; violet flowers, 8 cm (3 in).

C. speciosus; hardy corm; large flowers in shades of lilac-blue, or white, 13 cm (5 in).

Cyclamen hederifolium (*C. neapolitanum*); hardy tuber; nodding pink or white flowers, 10 cm (4 in).

Nerine bowdenii; hardy bulb; heads of pink flowers, 30–45 cm (12–18 in).

Winter

EVERGREENS
Hedera (ivies); see 'Foliage plants' (Summer).

Erica carnea and *E.* × *darleyensis* varieties (winter heathers); *Sedum* and *Sempervivum*; *Euonymus fortunei* varieties; and *Carex morrowii* 'Evergold'; see 'Plants for Permanent Display' for details.

BULBS, CORMS AND TUBERS
Crocus chrysanthus varieties; hardy corm; yellow, cream, blue and white, 8 cm (3 in).

C. laevigatus 'Fontenayi'; hardy corm; lilac-blue, 8 cm (3 in).

Cyclamen coum; hardy tuber; nodding ruby-red or rose-pink flowers, 8 cm (3 in).

Eranthis hyemalis (winter aconite); hardy tuber; yellow buttercup flowers, 10 cm (4 in).

Galanthus nivalis (snowdrop); hardy bulb; single and double flowered forms, 13 cm (5 in).

G. elwesii (Turkish snowdrop); hardy bulb; large flowered species, 15–20 cm (6–8 in).

Iris danfordiae; hardy bulb; lemon-yellow, 8 cm (3 in).

I. histrioides 'Major'; hardy bulb; sky-blue, large flowers, 10 cm (4 in).

I. reticulata varieties; hardy bulb; blue, violet and purple-red, 13 cm (5 in).

Narcissus bulbocodium (hoop petticoat daffodil); hardy bulb; golden-yellow, 10 cm (4 in).

BUSHY PLANTS
Viola (winter-flowering pansy strains); hardy annual; various colours, 10–15 cm (4–6 in).

Spring

BULBS, CORMS AND TUBERS
Anemone blanda; hardy tuber; blue, pink, red and white, 10 cm (4 in).

Chionodoxa (glory of the snow); hardy bulb; blue flowers, 13 cm (5 in).

Crocus; hardy corm; various kinds, including *C. sieberi* 'Violet Queen' and *C. minimus* (violet-blue).

Hyacinthus (hyacinth); hardy bulb; rose-red, pink, lavender-blue, mauve and white, 20–30 cm (8–12 in).

Ipheon uniflorum; hardy bulb; violet-blue, 15 cm (6 in).

Muscari (grape hyacinth); hardy bulb; blue, 15 cm (6 in).

Narcissus (daffodil); hardy bulb; short-growing cyclamineus, triandrus and jonquilla hybrids, 15–30 cm (6–12 in).

Tulipa; hardy bulb; rock garden species and dwarf kaufmanniana and greigii hybrids, 10–20 cm (4–8 in).

BEDDING PLANTS
Bellis perennis (daisy); hardy perennial; double and single varieties, white, pink and red, 8–15 cm (3–6 in).

Cheiranthus (wallflower); various colours, dwarf varieties 15–30 cm (6–12 in).

Myosotis alpestris (forget-me-not); hardy biennial; blue flowers, 15–30 cm (6–12 in).

Primula (primrose and polyanthus); hardy perennials; various colours, 10–25 cm (4–10 in).

Viola (pansy); various colours, 10–15 cm (4–6 in).

PLANTS FOR PERMANENT DISPLAYS

Evergreen foliage plants

Asplenium trichomanes; evergreen fern, 8–15 cm (3–6 in).

Carex morrowii 'Evergold'; golden-leaved evergreen grass, 30 cm (1 ft).

Conifers; all slow-growing dwarf varieties are suitable; see 'Permanent planting schemes' chapter for suggestions.

Euonymus fortunei; silver, gold and pink variegated forms, 20–30 cm (8–12 in).

Heathers; golden and silvery foliage varieties of *Erica carnea, E × darleyensis* and *Calluna vulgaris,* 15–30 cm (6–12 in).

Festuca; evergreen grasses; *F. glauca* (silver-blue) and *F. scoparia* (green), 15–20 cm (6–8 in).

Hedera (ivies); as climbers and trailers, green-leaved or silver and golden variegated.

Phyllitis scolopendrium; evergreen fern, 20–30 cm (8–12 in).

Polypodium vulgare; evergreen fern, 30 cm (1 ft).

Sedum (stonecrop); many varieties with colourful leaf tints, 5–8 cm (2–3 in).

Sempervivum (houseleek); most have colourful leaf rosettes, 5–8 cm (2–3 in).

Spring flowers

TOUGH ROCK PLANTS AND DWARF SHRUBS

Alyssum saxatile; trailer, grey-green leaves and yellow flowers, 15–20 cm (6–8 in).

Arabis caucasica (*A. albida,* rock cress); trailer, white, 15 cm (6 in).

Armeria caespitosa (alpine thrift); cushion plant, pink flowers, 10 cm (4 in).

Aubrieta (aubretias); trailer; red, pink, mauve, blue, 10–20 cm (4–8 in).

Azalea; dwarf evergreen varieties are suitable; must have lime-free compost.

Berberis stenophylla 'Corallina Compacta'; dwarf evergreen shrub, orange flowers, eventually 45 cm (18 in) but slow growing.

Daphne retusa; dwarf evergreen shrub, fragrant mauve-white flowers, eventually 60 cm (2 ft) but very slow.

Iberis sempervirens (candytuft); bushy, white flowers, 15–20 cm (6–8 in).

Phlox (alpine phlox); trailer; red, pink, mauve, lilac and white varieties of *P. subulata* and *P. douglasii,* 10–20 cm (4–8 in).

Rhododendron; the tiniest dwarf species and varieties are suitable; lime-free compost essential.

Summer flowers

TOUGH ROCK PLANTS

Achillea; trailers, mostly yellow flowers and silver-grey leaves, 13 cm (5 in).

Armeria maritima (sea thrift); cushion plant, red, pink or white flowers, 15 cm (6 in).

Calluna vulgaris; summer-flowering heathers, purple-red, pink and white, 15–30 cm (6–12 in).

Campanula (bell flower); trailers, blue or white flowers, 10–20 cm (4–8 in).

Dianthus (pinks); cushion plants; alpine species and modern border 'pinks', pink or white flowers, 10–25 cm (4–10 in) according to variety.

Helianthemum (rock rose); trailers; yellow, orange, red, pink and white, 15 cm (6 in).

Hypericum; dwarf shrubby alpine species are suitable, yellow flowers, 10–20 cm (4–8 in).

Lithospermum diffusum; shrubby trailer, blue flowers, 15 cm (6 in).

Oenothera missouriensis (evening primrose); trailer, huge yellow flowers, 20 cm (8 in).

Thymus drucei (*T. serpyllum,* thyme); aromatic trailer, pink or red flowers, 5 cm (2 in).

Veronica prostrata (speedwell); trailer, blue, 10 cm (4 in).

Autumn

ROCK PLANTS

Gentiana septemfida; trailer, blue flowers, 13 cm (5 in).

G. sino-ornata; trailer, blue flowers, 13 cm (5 in); lime-free compost essential.

Polygonum vacciniifolium; trailer, pink flowers, 16 cm (6 in).

See also autumn bulbs under 'Seasonal plants'.

Winter

Erica carnea (winter heather); crimson, pink and white (some with golden foliage), 15–25 cm (6–10 in).
E. × *darleyensis* (winter heather); as above.
See also winter-flowering bulbs under 'Seasonal plants'.

Specialist rock garden window box

Dianthus alpinus (alpine pink); rose-red summer flowers, 8 cm (3 in).
Gentiana verna (spring gentian); sky-blue flowers, 8 cm (3 in).
Juniperus communis 'Compressa'; one of the tiniest and loveliest dwarf conifers, spire-shaped 60 cm (2 ft) maximum after many years.

Primula auricula; yellow spring flowers, 10–15 cm (4–6 in).
P. marginata; lilac-blue, spring, 10 cm (4 in).
Saxifraga; cushion-forming 'kabschia' types (e.g. *S. burserana*), spring; and rosette-forming 'encrusted' types, summer; 8 cm (3 in).

Fruit, vegetables and herb suggestions

Note: no sizes are given for herbs, since these will be kept small and bushy by nipping off shoots for kitchen use:
Strawberries (especially alpine varieties); dwarf bush tomatoes, lettuce, radish and spring onions; basil, bay (eventually makes large shrub, but suitable for a while), chervil, chives, garlic, marjoram, mint, parsley, rosemary, sage, thyme.

INDEX